EXPERT HUMANS

EXPERT HUMANS

Critical Leadership Skills for a Disrupted World

By

Michael Jenkins

United Kingdom – North America – Japan
India – Malaysia – China

Emerald Publishing Limited
Howard House, Wagon Lane, Bingley BD16 1WA, UK

First edition 2021

Copyright © 2021 Michael Jenkins. Published under exclusive licence by Emerald
Publishing Limited.

Reprints and permissions service
Contact: permissions@emeraldinsight.com

No part of this book may be reproduced, stored in a retrieval system, transmitted
in any form or by any means electronic, mechanical, photocopying, recording or
otherwise without either the prior written permission of the publisher or a licence
permitting restricted copying issued in the UK by The Copyright Licensing Agency
and in the USA by The Copyright Clearance Center. Any opinions expressed in
the chapters are those of the authors. Whilst Emerald makes every effort to ensure
the quality and accuracy of its content, Emerald makes no representation implied
or otherwise, as to the chapters' suitability and application and disclaims any
warranties, express or implied, to their use.

British Library Cataloguing in Publication Data
A catalogue record for this book is available from the British Library

ISBN: 978-1-80071-261-4 (Print)
ISBN: 978-1-80071-260-7 (Online)
ISBN: 978-1-80071-262-1 (Epub)

ISOQAR certified
Management System,
awarded to Emerald
for adherence to
Environmental
standard
ISO 14001:2004.

Certificate Number 1985
ISO 14001

INVESTOR IN PEOPLE

This book is dedicated to Margaret Dunlop, a truly Expert Human.

ACKNOWLEDGEMENTS

I would like to thank my family for their invaluable ideas, insights and suggestions during the writing of Expert Humans: my wife Joyce for thinking things through with me, my daughter Maia for her superb advice and feedback, and my son Nat for his technical assistance. Thanks everyone!

I would also like to thank Andy Dunlop, Dr Robyn Wilson, Dr Vijayan Munusamy, and my agent Nick Wallwork for their unstinting support and encouragement. Thank you.

Michael Jenkins

Singapore, 2020

CONTENTS

List of Tables and Figures   xi

Author Biography   xiii

Introduction   xv

PART ONE   WHAT'S GOING ON?

Chapter 1   Disruption – Critical Leadership for a
            Disrupted World   3

Chapter 2   Purpose and Sustainability – Where Are We
            Heading?   17

Chapter 3   Impact – What Impact Will This Disruption
            Have on Humans and the Workplace?   33

PART TWO   HOW DO WE FIT IN?

Chapter 4   Drawing on Human Psychology   51

Chapter 5   Breaking New Ground – Introduction of the
            ACE Model   67

Chapter 6   Altruism in the Workplace   85

Chapter 7   Compassion in the Workplace   101

Chapter 8   Empathy in the Workplace   119

PART THREE   WHAT HAPPENS NEXT?

Chapter 9   What Do We Need to Stop, Start, or Continue?   141

Chapter 10   Where Do We Go from Here?   159

References   179

Index   187

LIST OF TABLES AND FIGURES

Part 1   Chapter 2
Table 1.   Purpose, Vision, and Mission   20
Fig. 1.   United Nations Sustainable Development Goals   23

Part 1   Chapter 3
Table 2.   Macrotrends Emerging over the Next Decade According
           to the World Business Council for Sustainable Development
           and Adapted by the Author   34
Table 3.   Sustainability Throughout the Kimberly–Clark Value
           Chain (from 2019 Global Kimberly–Clark Sustainability
           Report, Adapted by the Author)   44

Part 2   Chapter 4 & 5
Table 4.   Johari Window   63
Table 5.   List of Adjectives for Johari Window   63
Fig. 2.   The ACE Model   71
Fig. 3.   Share of Population with Mental or Substance Disorders,
           Male versus Female, 1990–2017. The Chart Shows the
           Situation in 2017   75
Fig. 4.   Prevalence by Mental and Substance Use Disorder,
           World, 2017   76

Part 2   Chapter 6
Table 6.   Types of Altruism   88
Table 7.   Altruism in Global Religions   90
Fig. 5.   Eisai's hhc Logo   96
Table 8.   Self-report Altruism Scale   98

Part 2   Chapter 7
Fig. 6.   Issues Confronting the Development of Compassion
           in the Workplace   105
Fig. 7.   Self-awareness/Self-compassion/Compassion   115

Part 2   Chapter 8
Table 9.   The Top 20 Most Empathetic Companies 2016   124
Table 10. Glassdoor Ratings for 2020   125
Table 11. Eight Key Actions to Promote Empathy in Organisations   129

Part 3   Chapter 9
Table 12. Critical Leadership Skills for a Disrupted
               World – Impact of ACE   155

Part 3   Chapter 10
Table 13. Rate of Automation: Division of Labour as Share
               of Hours Spent (%)   173

AUTHOR BIOGRAPHY

Michael Jenkins was born and spent his early years in Malaysia. He graduated from Durham University in Chinese Studies followed by postgraduate studies in Japanese language, politics, and economics at Nanzan University, Nagoya, Japan (supported by a scholarship from the Rotary Foundation for International Understanding) after which he worked for Toyota Motor Corporation for four years as a Motor Analyst in the Overseas Planning Department.

Returning to the United Kingdom in 1988, he worked at the University of Bath as Director of the Foreign Languages Centre where he established and taught on the UK's first PG Diploma in Japanese and English Interpreting and Translation. In 2001, after two years with INSEAD in France as Regional Director, Japan and Korea, he returned to Asia as Director of INSEAD Executive Education in Singapore. He subsequently took on the role of Managing Director of the Center for Creative Leadership Asia Pacific and in 2009 he joined Roffey Park Institute in the United Kingdom as CEO. Moving back to Singapore, he joined the Human Capital Leadership Institute as CEO in July 2018 before moving to set up a new company, Expert Humans in April 2020.

The United Kingdom's *HR Magazine* named him as one of the United Kingdom's Most Influential Thinkers in Human Resources in 2013 and again in 2016. He served as a member of the Institute of Human Resource Professionals Board in Singapore from 2018 to 2020 and in July 2020 he joined the UK-based FutureWork Forum (which explores the working world of tomorrow) as a Partner. He is a regular contributor at conferences in Singapore and abroad where he specialises in topics such as humanising the workplace, new thinking in leadership development, the Future of Work, and sustainability.

INTRODUCTION

We live in a disrupted world where change is rapid and relentless. Technological advances and an acceleration in adverse global climate change underscore a massive quickening of transformation and disruption. Added to this we
have far-reaching global health challenges, ongoing and persistent inequality
of many kinds and an all-pervasive crisis of trust in human institutions across
the political, social, and business landscape. In *Expert Humans*, we take a look
at all these disruptors and ask: what are the critical leadership skills needed to
chart a course to benefit human beings now – and into the future?

Change has always been part of the human experience, but it is the speed
of current disruption that marks the changes we are going through now
as being fundamentally different to the changes of the past. At the same
time, there is growing unease around our ability *as humans* – to keep up.
This book aims to take the reader through a brief history of fundamental
human qualities and core attributes, pointing out along the way the 'hidden
gems' of what it means to be human and the nature of the human experience, while also making specific reference to what it means to be a working
individual, in the workplace, in the here and now. *Expert Humans* looks
at important aspects of human psychology as well as suggesting practical
ways to make the world of work a better place, starting with improving the
quality of our leadership.

In writing *Expert Humans*, I have tried to combine the knowledge I have
accumulated over three decades spent in people development to propose some
new approaches to how we work together in organisations. In the book, we
scrutinise the often overlooked and under-emphasised human attributes of
altruism, compassion, and empathy via the ACE model, arguing strongly that
these are fantastic elements at our disposal if only we knew more about how
to make the most of them. Stories about how organisations have adopted a
more human approach to business and work life afford examples of what is
possible, and they give the reader the impetus to get started on developing a
more human workplace for themselves. We also look at concrete actions we

can take to develop some of our under-utilised human skills to complement the professional and technical skills we already possess. The book draws on a broad set of data sources – economic, financial, social, and demographic – to strengthen the evidence base for change and to give those sceptics the reassurance that the deep human skills we examine in the book are far from soft and 'nice-to-have': in fact, they are going to come strongly to the fore in the years ahead as technology accelerates the replacement and augmentation of humans and the clamour for action around sustainable business becomes ever louder. We will also consider how strengthening our human skills, as humans, benefits not only organisations in terms of equality, creativity, innovation, talent attraction, and talent retention, but critically, individuals themselves are less likely to suffer the mental ill-health that frequently results from working in a toxic or psychologically unsafe workplace.

The book closes by underscoring the growing awareness across the world that digital disruption is less about robots and chatbots and more about real people and that climate change and the concomitant encroachment on animal habitats and the increased potential for animal to human viral transmission – were wrought by the action of humans and in turn, must be arrested by humans.

The good news is that the development of more human organisations and leaders is attracting an increasing amount of interest and support. Adding fuel to calls for substantive change have been the disruptive events of recent times, giving us a rare window of opportunity that we should try to use to everyone's advantage – in other words, we should act before disillusionment about the true potential for change sets in. Calls to re-imagine the future of work, advocacy for sustainable and responsible business plus the eruption of anger around racial equality should give us all hope that despite the enormity of the tasks at hand, the biggest disruptors of the day can be tackled head on by talented people and the deep human skills of altruism, compassion, and empathy.

PART ONE

WHAT'S GOING ON?

1

DISRUPTION – CRITICAL LEADERSHIP FOR A DISRUPTED WORLD

A brief look at where we are in terms of technological and digital disruption and what's likely to happen in the next five years or so.

- The tyranny of the algorithm.

- Dehumanisation.

- Are we heading into an 'AI winter'? If so, is this an opportunity in time for us to catch up on our development into 'Expert Humans'? If not, is this the time to accelerate that same development?

- Jobs of the future – how these will require 'Expert Humans'.

- Corporate psychopaths and the erosion of trust.

Disruption comes in many forms. It can mean 'preventing a system, process or event from continuing as usual or as expected' (Cambridge English Dictionary). In business, disruption means the action of completely changing the traditional way in which an industry or market is operated – through the introduction of new methods or technology.

We are living in a time of multifaceted disruption. Technological advances and digital transformation wrought by artificial intelligence (AI) are examples of changes that impact our lives in ways that were unimaginable even a short time ago. But that is not all. Our world is undergoing disruption to its very core. Sustainability of the planet is at the forefront of public discourse: it has taken on an urgency and intensity of a kind that we have not seen before. We are at a pivotal point ecologically but also, I would argue, we are entering an age where people are questioning the fundamentals both of what it means to be human and how we interact with each other at a profound level. Privacy and individual protections have suffered an irreversible assault due to the intrusiveness of social media and the surge in populist sentiment around the world. These are disruptions too.

What this all means is that our lives are being changed in ways that are both obvious and covert. In *Expert Humans*, I will set out an agenda which advocates a change in human behaviour to benefit us as a species at a macro- and micro-level.

THE TYRANNY OF THE ALGORITHM

Let us zero in on one major source of disruption coming from AI: the algorithm. The author of *The Master Algorithm*, Pedro Domingos (2017), quoted in the World Economic Forum article *Artificial Intelligence can make our societies more equal: here's how* – makes a good point:

> *People worry that computers will get too smart and take over the world, but the real problem is that they're too stupid and they've already taken over the world.*

An algorithm consists of a set of procedures followed to produce a specific outcome. In AI terms, algorithms carry out computational tasks based on defined parameters – and the integrity of algorithms as we perceive them today are influenced by the humans who put them together in the first place. And where humans are involved, the potential for unintended consequences is huge. Chris Brahm of Bain & Co (2018) has noted that AI can lead to a number of risks that we need to consider carefully: they can create hidden errors; they can lead to a loss of critical thinking; they can open up new hazards; they can cause a loss of control. But most significantly, they can unwittingly institutionalise bias and contribute to a loss of empathy. We will explore these issues in more detail later in the book but for now, it is worth noting that the effect on humans has already started. Some might call it the tyranny of the algorithm.

What we do know is that opinions of AI and disruption are a complicated mosaic. We have entrepreneurs and visionaries such as Elon Musk heralding the end of work as we know it, who believe 'AI will make jobs kind of pointless', and are looking ahead with cautious but gloomy pessimism. Then there are leaders like Jack Ma who, while seeing AI and technology as a huge opportunity, believe 'man can never make another man. Computers only have chips, men have hearts'.

Research has shown professionals in recently automated organisations have mixed attitudes to the new technology in their lives. A 2020 survey from edtech company MindEdge/Skye Learning found that 76% of respondents who had had AI, robot workers and analytics introduced in their workplace felt this technology had 'made their lives easier', while 69% said it had a positive impact on overall company morale. So far, so good. However, while almost half of those surveyed said they 'weren't at all worried' about being replaced by technology, a similar number (57%) agreed that 'robots and advanced automation are bad for American workers'. This shows the degree to which workers are conflicted over AI and the dehumanisation of labour – tech makes life easier, but it's also bad?

Fear about job losses connects at a profound level with the notion of core human identity. The thinker Dan Pink has written extensively about what constitutes motivation in humans and has concluded that three things are key. These are: purpose, autonomy and mastery. It is the aspect of mastery – the idea that people derive a sense of self-worth and identity as a result of being good at something – *and being recognised as good at that thing by others* – that fuels our particular anxiety about being replaced by the 'human' face of AI – robots. This anxiety has led to the publication of a number of reports from highly reputable organisations seeking to understand the future impact of AI on humans at work. And wherever you get your numbers, the estimates are astronomical: '133 million new jobs will be created, but 75 million jobs are likely to be eliminated', according to a World Economic Forum report in 2016. And a McKinsey Global Institute report (2017) says, 'between 400 million and 800 million individuals could be displaced by automation and will need to find new jobs by 2030', though as many jobs – if not more – could be created. And there are many others. Forward-facing thinkers like to talk about 'jobs that don't exist yet' as one way to assuage what might be in store for us. The question is: what form will these jobs take, and what can humans do to prepare themselves to land one? What new skills might humans need to develop in order to meet the challenges ahead?

So, this concept then of 'job churn', in which more jobs are created to replace those that are eliminated, could provide some comfort. What we know for sure is that digital disruption is creating challenges in every sector. The key lies in identifying those skills that make us human and drawing those out to the best of our abilities.

In their 2020 *Randstad Talent Trends Report: Looking to soft skills*, Randstad highlighted the importance of talent fluidity, that is, professionals who can shape their skills to complement AI, automation and changing company needs. Commenting on her company's report, Rebecca Henderson, Randstad's CEO of global businesses, emphasised the fact that digitalisation has 'redefined the skills that are most important for employees to possess' and said it was important that organisations 'reskill staff to keep up with changing technology and bolster the soft skills that only humans can possess'.

It follows then, as we stand on the cusp of the third decade of the twenty-first century, that technological and digital disruption will continue to transform the world of work at every level. To many, this represents not only a threat to jobs, but a threat to what it means to be human. For many, there's a fear not only of job loss, but of an irrelevance that will make it close to impossible for large sectors of society to ever find work again. If careers and identity are inextricably entwined, what does it mean to face down a future in which the work we do is basically useless? We will return to this question again when we consider what human skills we need to dial up – and what human behaviours in the global workplace might need to be dialled down or even eliminated.

The key point is that humans are going to have to work harder at being not just experts in their chosen (technical) field – but at becoming expert at being human too.

We know that AI is imperfect. The algorithms which characterise AI are vulnerable to errors and are vulnerable to hackers as well. This means the human aspect (for checks and balances) may actually become more, not less, important even as progress continues to be made to eliminate bias from AI. 'Navigating the impact of robotics, automation, and AI is a pillar of modern business operations that will take time and experience for business leaders and employees to understand', said Jefferson Flanders, CEO of MindEdge Learning (in 2020).

> *American workers are continuing to uncover exactly how they feel about robotics and automation in the workplace. But regardless of how they may feel, technology is inexorably transforming the U.S. workforce – and employers and workers need to prepare for it.*

We can also discern mixed feelings in the world of Cloud Security. A 2020 report by the Ponemon Institute entitled 'Staffing the IT Security Function in the Age of Automation' and reported on by Scott Ikeda of CPO magazine, found that while 74% of IT security decision-makers agree that automation frees up IT staff to focus more on 'serious vulnerabilities and overall security network security', only 40% of respondents believe automation leads to a reduction in human error. On top of this, half of respondents believe automation will actually make jobs more complex, and 54% said automation will never replace 'human intuition and hands-on experience'. An even larger percentage (74%) report that automation is not capable of certain tasks, up from 69% the previous year.

And in an article in the *Financial Times* in November 2019, "Workers can learn to love Artificial Intelligence," the journalist Gillian Tett described a study by Google in which a research team from the company discovered that modern office workers tend to make a mental distinction between 'core' work – or jobs they identify with – and 'peripheral' work – work that does not contribute to their wellbeing or happiness. As Gillian goes on to say: 'Office workers will readily use AI to replace peripheral work. But they resist this for core work'.

This demonstrates how attitudes to AI and technology are not only complex, but susceptible to large shifts year on year. What this means is that while improvements in AI and technology might well be exponential, the human dimension in all of this is likely to be lumpy, pattern-less, and unpredictable. In other words, the antithesis of the algorithm.

DEHUMANISATION

These days, without even trying, it would be easy to pass an entire day devoid of human-to-human interaction.

Self-checkouts; ATMs; Starbucks pre-ordered for pick-up; automated machines for train tickets to and from work. In 2019, the rideshare platform Uber unveiled the 'quiet preferred' option on their app, allowing passengers to choose whether or not they want their driver to talk. Even our choices of music are made for us, generated by an algorithm and curated by streaming platforms. It's no great secret AI has seamlessly dismantled the day-to-day interactions we have with other people – often so fast and with such convenience we hardly have time to notice. These days, I'll find myself more surprised by having to interact with a real-life customer service representative than the reverse. Without question, AI has made life more convenient – and people will continue to make use of these conveniences as long as they serve them.

And at the same time, AI is helping to erode some of the 'weak-tie networks' we all have that are important for mental wellbeing: these refer to the interactions we have with other humans who we know but don't *really* know. These include the barista who knows our order but not necessarily our name; the school bus driver who picks up our kids each morning who waves and smiles as she pulls away; the friendly guy in the local 7-Eleven who cracks a joke about you calling in (every night) at 11 p.m. to buy a bar of chocolate. Every time a weak-tie event occurs (you smile, the other person smiles back) – your brain is bathed in feel-good chemicals. It's important we protect these precious moments.

There are also cultural and generational differences when it comes to AI. At the supermarket recently, I witnessed an older gentleman struggling with the self-checkout machine. 'We should get a 10% discount for having to check the groceries out ourselves', he joked with the attendant who came to his aid. On the other end of the spectrum, those of us with Gen-Z or even Millennial children will know how keen they are on automated, self-service systems – and how they will go out of their way to use them.

In a 2020 Zapier report, it was found almost all Gen-Z (95%) and Millennial (91%) respondents were willing to automate at least part of their jobs. What's interesting are the reasons behind this openness: of those who said 'yes', the majority only wanted to automate parts of their jobs if it meant more flexible work hours (61%) and allowed them more time to spend with loved ones (54%). These are uniquely human motivations. It seems, among this generation in particular, there's already an instinctive understanding of how AI can weave through our working day to boost and bolster personal lives rather than inhibiting or infringing upon them. I argue that even in the self-service age, even among these digital natives who are perfectly comfortable going from one automated service to another, we are all still intensely social creatures who need person-to-person interactions.

In many ways, we human beings are already half-ceded to the digital world. This is nothing new. Since the advent of the first computer, humans have had a morbid curiosity with the notion of atomisation; how technology drives us further from each other, nor closer. This rapid, seemingly unstoppable hold AI has on our lives makes the case for Expert Humans even more urgent. In the fast-moving age of digital disruption, we may have to take a step back/slow down before we can move forwards. If we want to talk about dehumanisation – that is, the removal of characteristics or attributes that make us people – we also need to establish what we think of as 'human' in the first place. As our daily interactions are transformed, we need a new social contract to match.

It's a mistake to believe things like altruism, empathy, and compassion are somehow innate. They don't happen by accident. Human skills, like any others, need to be honed. We will explore this in some depth later in the book when we consider the application of the simple ACE framework (Altruism, Compassion, and Empathy).

DEHUMANISATION AND THE RISE OF THE CHATBOT

Nowadays, chatbots are ubiquitous: Meena. Stella. Mya. Unsurprisingly for computer programmes designed to mimic human interaction, many of these bots are given human names.

There are many examples of chatbots used for altruistic purposes. The Endurance chatbot, for example, helps those who suffer from dementia and Alzheimer's. By identifying typical confusions and diversions in conversation, the Endurance chatbot aims to provide patients with companionship and conversational signals to bring those with short-term memory loss back into the present day without the embarrassment and distress of messing up 'real' human conversation.

Then there's U-Report – a social media tool and bot service run by UNICEF. The U-Report provides polls, data, and alerts to participants about mental health, infectious diseases, sanitation, water, education, and more to young people, many of whom are then linked with an on-the-ground U-Reporter if they want to seek further support. By 2020, the tool had 304,355 U-Reporters in 60 different countries, with a global reach of 8 million people. During Hurricanes, Irma, Jose, and Maria, U-Reporters were able to send messages on how to stay safe and provide advice to 8,500 people in just 48 hours.

One of the biggest users of chatbots today is the banking industry which has embraced them with great enthusiasm, insisting to finance sector workers that such innovations enable them to be able to devote time to more people-oriented things.

What is not so well-known, but is emerging as an unintended consequence, is that staff who previously dealt with phone calls about relatively trivial matters – are reporting the first instances of what we could call a gradual decline in empathy for the customer – precisely because they have yielded those traditional interactions to a chatbot. They talk about 'feeling more distant from the customer'. The case might be overstated or overblown, but it is interesting to consider the longer-term ramifications of such seemingly sensible innovations.

And still, when it comes to complex enquiries, many customers want to talk to a real person. How much time have we spent on virtual customer service helplines – or typing our enquiries into chatbot boxes – going around and around in circles, just longing to 'talk to a human being'? So often, a complicated problem can be solved almost immediately through the simple act of a conversation. No matter how smooth the tech, there are some things that cannot be replaced by robots. At least, not yet.

The HR or Human Resources function has also joined in the race to embrace tech. Internal staff enquiries about payroll matters or leave entitlement have been automated for some time now, leaving HR people more time to interact with the people they serve.

But does it really? People I work with profess to a deep scepticism over the 'chatbots-mean-more-time-for-humans' narrative. For many, the primary objective is to save costs – and that means reducing headcount. Others say – without a hint of irony – that giving HR staff more time to interact with the people in the organisation – is not necessarily a great idea in and of itself. Why? Well, the real question is not one of more time in an absolute sense – but actually ensuring that the time that *does* become available – is spent on constructive, meaningful, empathic, and compassionate conversations. So, allowing more time for HR people to talk to staff when they are not adequately equipped to have those conversations – is frankly quite pointless. We should celebrate the fact that AI – chatbots and all – offer a never-seen-before opportunity for HR professionals to spend time improving and honing their people skills, but we also need to take responsibility for ensuring that the HR people themselves are suitably prepared and equipped.

At Singapore's DBS Bank, for example, the cheerily named JIM (short for 'Jobs Intelligence Maestro') has been instrumental in revolutionising the organisation's recruitment process, taking over psychometric profiling, CV screening, data collation and other repetitive tasks that previously fell to

HR professionals. Developed in 2018, Jim has slashed the average candidate screening time from 32 minutes to 8 minutes. That's 24 minutes of time per candidate, or 2.7 months over a two-year span. Looking at the time saved through the implementation of AI, it's easy to see why leaders get excited about the possibilities: imagine what we could do with those extra hours, days, and months that were previously spent crossing t's and dotting i's. In a 2019 presentation mentioned by *People Matters* magazine, Susan Cheong, DBS' Head of Talent Acquisition, said that the beauty of JIM lay in freeing up her team to spend 'quality time' with 'hiring managers to understand their business needs without feeling they need to fill vacancies within the same amount of time'. Interestingly, however, Cheong added that nothing could replace the 'face-to-face' interview stage of recruitment. It seems even at this sophisticated stage of AI in recruitment, that irreplaceable human element must enter play at the last inning.

The crucial thing is to ensure that this happens.

ARE WE HEADING INTO AN AI WINTER?

The term 'AI winter' comes from the nomenclature around the history of artificial intelligence and is analogous to the notion of a nuclear winter. It references the phenomenon of AI development occurring in a kind of 'fits and starts' way: one minute there is hype around amazing possibilities for AI and then the next minute the excitement dissipates, funding gets terminated and then some years later, interest is rekindled, and the buzz starts again.

Some observers think that following what is clearly an exponential burst of AI-related activity in the last decade, we might be on the verge of a new AI winter. Much of what we are currently experiencing in terms of AI advancement after all comes directly as a result of significantly enhanced computing power: our computers are simply able to process data faster than ever before.

As circumstantial evidence that an AI winter might be upon us, it is interesting to note the stop-start nature of robot development. Are the robots perhaps 'in retreat'? Research and development into humanoid form robots appears to have been curtailed for many of the pioneers in this field. Honda stopped development of its humanoid ASIMO robot in June 2018. Perhaps one of the ongoing challenges is creating a robot that can walk up a flight of stairs! Joking apart, the stage seems to be set for robots to be less human in form and more functional – sitting on kitchen tabletops and desks, for example, or showing up in other forms and formats. Interestingly though, Sony has decided to bring back its AIBO dog robot after a hiatus of 12 years – and this version apparently is designed to foster empathy and compassion with its owner!

If we are indeed heading into a period where the pace of advancement in AI is potentially going to slow down, might this be an ideal time to play catch-up in terms of human skills development in organisations?

JOBS OF THE FUTURE

In the current climate, there's much discussion around how to attract 'top talent' in order to maximise competition and profit. I'd like to posit the notion that what constitutes 'talent' has changed and needs redefinition. In a 2013 interview with *Vanity Fair*, Elon Musk was asked about the 'biggest mistake' of his career. He had the following to say:

> *The biggest mistake, in general, I've made, is to put too much of a weighting on someone's talent and not enough on their personality. And I've made that mistake several times. I think it actually matters whether somebody has a good heart, it really does.*

While I'd agree with Musk's assessment, I would take it further and suggest personality *is* a talent, one that will become increasingly essential for the future of jobs, whatever it holds. When Musk talks of recruiting people with 'good hearts', can we assume he means loyal, trustworthy, kind individuals? People with integrity, who can put themselves in their colleagues' shoes and show a generosity of spirit even when mistakes are made and the going gets particularly tough? Or is Musk referring to EQ (Emotional Intelligence Quotient)? It's probably a combination of all the above.

What I'd like to look towards in the following pages, however, is a way to define more solidly these so-called 'good hearts'. For jobs of the future I'd like to move away from this idea of a 'good personality' as a rare abstraction – a stroke of luck found only in once-in-a-blue-moon candidates – to a talent/skill in itself that can be drawn out, honed, developed and even taught. Through this, we stand to create a taskforce of Expert Humans who can deploy their carefully developed skills – altruism, compassion, empathy – in all areas of life and through this, create trusting and trusted organisations.

And so, I think that we will start to see a gradual evolution in terms of the importance of these 'soft skills' over the next five years and indeed in the years to come. LinkedIn's study (by B. Anderson, 2020) of the most in-demand skills for 2020 would seem to underscore the trend that we are seeing (which was also noted in 2019) and suggests that 'Expert Human Skills' will play a significant role in them:

'Soft skills'

1. Creativity
2. Persuasion
3. Collaboration
4. Adaptability
5. Emotional intelligence.

'Hard skills'

1. Blockchain
2. Cloud computing
3. Analytical reasoning
4. Artificial Intelligence
5. UX design
6. Business analysis
7. Affiliate marketing
8. Sales
9. Scientific computing
10. Video production.

The 2019 report noted: 'The rise of AI is making soft skills increasingly important as they are precisely the skills that cannot be automated'. The 2020 report underscored this with: '… slipping in at No. 5 is a newcomer, emotional intelligence, a skill important in just about every role'.

It would seem that developing 'Expert Humans' – developing those human skills that cannot be automated – is the way to go.

And such a message comes through in reports such as the 2020 World Economic Forum's *The Future of Jobs: Employment, Skills and Workforce Strategy for the Fourth Industrial Revolution* too:

> *Overall, social skills – such as persuasion, emotional intelligence and teaching others – will be in higher demand across industries than narrow technical skills, such as programming or equipment operation and control.*

I believe that the development of these human skills will form the bedrock of the jobs of the future. If we are fortunate, they will also start to change the fundamental nature of organisations themselves. There will be knock-on, positive effects, whereby underserved organisational qualities such as good governance and corporate morality will stand to benefit from the actions of leaders who practice the human skills of the Expert Human. Let me give you some examples.

In a seminar I was giving to a group of people from a global insurance company about compassion in the workplace, I was unexpectedly interrupted by a male participant who said:

> *Michael, I kind of, get this compassion thing. I only have one question to ask you. And that is – when do you switch it [compassion] off? I mean, when you've sweet-talked people and played nice with them, given them plenty of chances – and they still won't do what you want them to do – isn't that when you switch it [compassion] off?*

I was momentarily taken aback and then I said: 'Compassion isn't something you switch on or off. Compassion is just – *there*. I am not sure we are actually talking about the same thing'. The man looked dissatisfied with my reply and thereafter, mentally checked-out of the session, throwing his arm over the back of his chair and staring blankly into the middle distance. I finished the session and as I was clearing up, putting my laptop and handouts into my backpack, the two HR colleagues who had invited me in to give the talk, stayed back. One of them said: 'We're very sorry about our colleague – we hope he didn't offend you'. I reassured them that it takes quite a lot to offend me and, therefore, they should not worry at all. They then went on to say that the man in question was – at that point in time – the subject of not one, but two separate cases of bullying and intimidation of other colleagues in the company. And at that point in the conversation I thought it was my turn to ask a question: 'And so then, if I might ask, comes a bigger question: if this man is a bully, why does your organisation tolerate such behaviour?' The two people gave each other a knowing look. I decided to hazard a guess. 'Do you tolerate him and his ways because he's your top earner? Someone who wins business and brings in the dollars?' They looked down and then around the room for a moment before finally nodding. Yes, that was the case. He was their star business performer. I waited a moment and then said:

> I guess you need to think about whether you want your company
> to be the kind of place where people are allowed to go about their
> work and their lives in this particular way. It's a cultural issue for
> the organisation as well as an issue at the level of the individual. It's
> an ethical and moral challenge.

I might have added that failure to address these issues results in the erosion of psychological safety and the destruction of trust.

I am sure that such stories will not surprise you. We have all at some point in our working lives come into contact with people who are bullies – some might call the more extreme examples of such people, corporate psychopaths. We all know who they are: charming and very often highly intelligent, they will block, obstruct or even destroy people unlucky enough to come into their orbit if those people represent competition to them or if they look like they might slow them down as they climb the corporate ladder. Fortunately for the rest of us, such people will eventually get found out, because, like their non-corporate counterparts, the serial killers, they always end up making mistakes – usually when they have run out of energy to keep up the façade of being someone they aren't.

Another data point to underscore the importance of human skills in corporate life: in the aftermath of the Global Financial Crisis of 2008–2009, governments around the world took it upon themselves to tighten governance and financial regulation with the intention of stopping a catastrophic incident like the financial crash happening again. A few years later, the well-respected Edelman Trust Barometer reported data that suggested no amount of regulation and tightening of the rules was likely to result in any significant improvement in corporate trust and that in its view, the key to improving trust lay in changing the fundamental cultural fabric of the organisation.

In other words, you can try implementing rules, but the fact remains that human beings are remarkably adept at getting around the rules – any rules. So, the answer to better ethics and morality in companies and organisations is less about regulating them and much more about ensuring that the human beings who lead these organisations are ethical and trustworthy. More recently, in the 2020 Edelman Trust Barometer (its 20th annual trust and credibility survey, conducted across a number of institutions, sectors, and geographies, and surveying more than 34,000 respondents across 28 countries), Antoine Harary, the President of Edelman Intelligence, had this to say:

> *After tracking 40 global companies over the past year through our Edelman Trust Management framework we've learned that ethical drivers such as integrity, dependability and purpose drive close to 76 percent of the trust capital of business, while competence accounts for only 24 percent .... Trust is undeniably linked to doing what is right. The battle for trust will be fought on the field of ethical behaviour.*

Trust is in short supply in our world today.

And I believe that the development of truly 'Expert Human' skills has got to be one of the biggest enablers of trust-building. We will explore this further in the chapters to come.

2

PURPOSE AND SUSTAINABILITY – WHERE ARE WE HEADING?

- What ever happened to Purpose? A reflection on the critical role of purpose in building a sustainable future.

- How can Purpose be strengthened? Where do Expert Humans come in?

- How can leaders and managers use an Expert Humans mindset to advance the sustainability agenda – and what does such a mindset look like?

WHAT EVER HAPPENED TO PURPOSE? A REFLECTION ON THE CRITICAL ROLE OF PURPOSE IN BUILDING A SUSTAINABLE FUTURE

It was following one of the last major global disruptions – the Global Financial Crisis of 2007–2008 – that the concept of Purpose and its centrality in organisational life really came to the fore. People wanted – and needed – reassurance about the meaning of work, given the tumult of those years, the wrecking of economies around the world and the collapse of trust in the banks and the banking system. Media pundits, government officials, and financial experts told us that lessons needed to be learned and that new practices should be put in place to avoid such chaos in the future. All good stuff. Yet The Edelman Trust Barometer, which publishes an annual report on brand and reputation around the world, reported in no uncertain terms that new legislation had had little or no effect on improving people's experience of, or trust in, financial services companies in the post-Global Financial Crash period. This is doubly concerning given the earlier introduction of the Sarbanes–Oxley Act of 2002 which was signed into law by George W. Bush to ensure integrity around corporate financial reporting, as well as to regulate accountancy firms. Sarbanes–Oxley came in the wake of the Enron scandal of 2000 (involving the accountancy firm Arthur Anderson) as well as other corporate misdemeanours perpetrated by companies such as World-Com and Tyco. So despite the miserable experience that many people went through at that time as a result of the unethical behaviour of certain parts of the banking sector, many financial institutions did not mend their ways or try particularly hard to change the dismal public view of banks in general.

THE PURPOSE-AND-MEANING VACUUM

So what went wrong? Well, governments responded to the financial crisis by deciding that more governance, more rules, and more regulation was what was needed when in fact what was needed was a root and branch change in corporate culture and behaviour. The unethical events and destruction of trust (caused by Enron, WorldCom, Tyco, Lehmann Brothers et al.) effectively created a 'purpose-and-meaning vacuum'. The good thing is that many thoughtful people have sought to overcome this purpose-and-meaning vacuum by deliberately placing Purpose centre stage in their writing on societal change, as well as in the leadership and organisational programmes that many of them, as experts on human capital, offer. They insist, quite rightly, that Purpose lies at the heart of everything. And yet we still seem to fall victim to what we could call patterns of disruption (like the Global Financial Crisis) that destroy many things and that eat away at Purpose. The attention people appear to give to Purpose seems to ebb and flow, coming into vogue when things are bad and then falling out of fashion once we have reverted to the old ways of doing things, until things go badly wrong again and we return, once again, to Purpose for inspiration and comfort. As a topic of discussion, therefore, Purpose is vulnerable to these shifting patterns. That is why, given the catastrophe that is COVID-19 and the surge of outrage around the world about racial inequality, we need to come back again to Purpose and ensure, to the extent that we can, that it is not side-lined and forgotten. The disruptive world we are living in now needs as many anchor-points as it is realistic to have – and I believe Purpose is one of these.

THINKING ABOUT PURPOSE

Writers such as Dan Pink advanced our thinking about Purpose when he used it to create an explanation for what motivates human beings. In Pink's book *Drive*, he explains how Purpose, together with Mastery (the idea of everyone wanting to be recognised as being good at something) and Autonomy (the idea that human beings like to be allowed independence to make their own decisions about things) – all combine to provide the basic elements underpinning human motivation. It is something that moves way beyond monetary gain – in fact, money hardly figures at all in the equation. So when did Purpose in organisations first come to the fore and where did the concept originate? What *is* Purpose? As the rapper Logic points out:

> *Just because you got money doesn't mean you're gonna be happy, and just 'cuz you can buy everything in the world doesn't mean you're gonna find your purpose.*

It's clear that Purpose can mean a lot of different things to different people, but for now I would like to focus on Purpose in a work context and then on Purpose in the broader setting of sustainability. As we will see, there are important connections between these two manifestations of Purpose.

PURPOSE IN A WORK CONTEXT: WHY ARE WE HERE, DOING WHAT WE'RE DOING?

Purpose appears frequently in discussions about an organisation's strategy or as part of strategic planning. Interestingly, many organisations conflate purpose with those other often cited things, mission and vision. But they are all different. With Purpose, one of the best ways I can think of both to define purpose in an organisational context and to set it apart from other strategic questions, is to think of Purpose as being the answer to the question: *Why are we here, doing what we're doing?* In other words, what is it that matters most to us and that won't really change, if at all, over time? Purpose is best thought of as a 'whole life thing' whereas vision and mission can change – and their time horizons can change.

One way of showing this is to group the various strategic elements into an at-a-glance table like Table 1 so that we can bring simplicity and clarity to these important concepts:

Table 1:   Purpose, Vision, and Mission.

	What Does it Mean?
Purpose	Why are we here, doing what we're doing?
Vision	What future do we want?
Mission	How will we get there?

In our disrupted world, we know that Purpose is one of the anchors that we can return to when the going gets rough. We might have to redefine our vision in light of various disruptions and revisit our mission when externalities oblige us to: this is precisely because the new situation we find ourselves in means we can no longer carry out our mission as originally intended. It might mean that because of forces beyond our control, we have to re-assess whether our vision – as it stands today – is actually realisable anymore. In the past, many companies have had to change their vision and mission without altering their fundamental purpose. Only rarely, I would argue, do companies change their purpose. One such example comes from India, where the 33-year old pharmaceuticals company Dr Reddy's Laboratories, decided over a decade ago to refine its purpose as being not just about bringing medicine to the people of India but about ensuring that the medicine itself was *affordable*, that is, bringing *affordable* medicine to the people of India. Fast-forward to 2017 and the company decided another dial-up of its purpose was needed. This has resulted in the company introducing the idea 'Good Health Can't Wait', which brilliantly broadens out its remit while at the same time introducing a new concept that combines speed, pace and agility. Something to reflect the changing times. They went further by stating:

Our business is based on a deep respect for people and the planet.

With this, the company was able to be crystal clear about where it stands. And if I might paraphrase, what the company is saying is: *The work we do is driven by humanity and sustainability.*

In his 2005 work written in association with the Roffey Park Institute in the United Kingdom: *Evaluating corporate purposes by the psychological contracts they produce*, Nigel Springett wrote:

Corporate purpose sits at the confluence of strategy and values. It expresses the company's fundamental value – the raison d'être *or overriding reason for existing.*

It is the end to which strategy is directed.

Nigel's thinking lent power to a movement which caused a major shift away from the notion that companies existed primarily to generate returns for their shareholders. So while many business schools built solid revenue streams in both MBA and Executive Education by – among other things – promoting the concept of maximising *shareholder* value, few companies today would feel comfortable mentioning this as the sole corporate strategic driver. Times have changed and the thinking has moved on. In fact, there have been tectonic shifts in attitudes with regards to the importance of purpose, which is a good thing. At the same time, many people feel that talk of 'building sustainability into the business model' as a more noble and thing to do, as a moral imperative, rather than talking about maximising shareholder value – lacks authenticity and truth. Hence the emergence of the word 'green-washing' (disinformation disseminated by an organisation so as to present an environmentally responsible public image). This means that if companies want to present green credentials, then they had better be ready to subject their words, deeds and actions to public scrutiny. And it should be said that making profits is not a bad thing per se – but it cannot be the only thing. Making profits needs to mean prosperity for all stakeholders. You can certainly champion Purpose *and* Profit. Nothing at all wrong with that. But not *just* Profit.

In his paper on sustainable business published by the FutureWork Forum entitled *Building Sustainability into the value chain*, part of a series for the European Foundation for Management Development, Rudi Plettinx of the Sustainability Centre Europe (recently renamed the SustenariGroup) puts it bluntly and forcefully:

All this should be a no-brainer for leaders who are attuned to thinking five, ten or twenty years into the future … if the policymakers and investors are measuring against green criteria today – it's a signal that everyone needs to put their sustainability lenses on …. The

change brought about by this new thinking will be a new generation
of leaders who are driven to build businesses with a purpose and
driven by prosperity rather than solely by profit and shareholder
value maximisation.

One person who is a standard bearer for sustainability – in this case, sustainability and food security – is the founder of Impossible Foods, Dr Pat Brown. His California-based company began experimenting with a synthesis of ingredients including heme (from soybeans) which, like hae-moglobin 'bleeds' (and sears, and smells, like haemoglobin). The Impossible Burger has undoubtedly made its mark on the restaurants around the world, with 1,400 outlets in the United States alone. In an interview with Joseph Hincks of *TIME* magazine during a visit to Hong Kong to explore the mar-ket for Impossible Food products in the territory, Dr Brown was asked what he thought about the possibility of Impossible Foods going interplanetary might be, and whether his technology could help humans to colonise Mars. Here's what he had to say:

> *Is our technology going to have a role in interplanetary colonisa-*
> *tion? Absolutely: it's going to make it unnecessary. People are seri-*
> *ously talking about going to Mars as the only way to save human*
> *civilisation from the catastrophic damage that we're going to do to*
> *Planet Earth. Look at a picture of Mars: that is a really sucky planet*
> *compared to Earth! No one should ever want to go to Mars. There's*
> *no air on Mars. And yet people are saying we've got to figure out a*
> *way to get to Mars so we can have a place to live when we've totally*
> *destroyed this planet. Well, the impact we're going to have makes it*
> *unnecessary to go to Mars by saving this planet and keeping it habit-*
> *able. We've got the best planet in the universe here. Let's not ruin it.*
> *(Hincks, 2018)*

Another company which can be seen as an exemplar organisation for sustainability that says what it will do and does what it says, is the Singa-pore- and Australia-based Singtel/Optus (the Singtel Group). This company has a highly public persona when it comes to sustainability leadership and its leaders are in lockstep when it comes to commitment to sustainable policies and actions – from the CEO through the CHRO and into the body politic of the organisation. In the group's sustainability reports for 2020, Simon Israel,

Chairman and the Group CEO Chua Sock Koong state: 'Solving the world's sustainability challenges requires the concerted and collective efforts of the Public–Private–People sectors. No individual or organisation can do it alone if we are to achieve scale and deliver a better and more sustainable future for all'. The Singtel Group has adopted the 17 SDGs of the United Nations (the Sustainable Development Goals) as foundational elements of its sustainability strategy. The SDGs are shown in Fig. 1.

This chart, with the 17 goals, forms the heart of the 2030 Agenda for Sustainable Development that was adopted by all member states of the UN in 2015. The key message underpinning the SDGs is that poverty and other global issues cannot be solved in isolation and must be tackled by parallel initiatives and programmes to address wellbeing and education, as well as reducing inequality of all kinds, generating positive economic outcomes and fighting climate change.

What many companies do is to figure out which of the 17 SDGs they wish to work on – given that it would be difficult to work on all them all at once! So in the case of Singtel, for example, the company focuses on 11 of the 17 SDGs: 3, 4, 5, 7, 8, 9, 10, 11, 12, 13, and 17 – which, taken as a whole, is an impressive ambition for any company. These SDGs complement the

Fig. 1:   United Nations Sustainable Development Goals.

company's stated four pillars for sustainability, namely Environment; People; Community and Marketplace & Customers. A look at Singtel's People section underscores the group's commitment to equality and to the development of young managers. Singtel is active in many areas of the value chain and the concomitant sustainability elements of it – and as such was as named the most well-governed and transparent company in Singapore for the fifth consecutive year in the Singapore Governance and Transparency Index 2019 and ranked as Australia's strongest brand in Brand Finance's Top 100.

Interestingly, Singtel like many Asian companies doesn't call out its Purpose, preferring instead to focus on its *Vision* – which in Singtel's case is 'To be Asia Pacific's best communications technology company'; its *Mission* – '*Breaking Barriers, Building Bonds* – We believe that the world is a better place when technology is used to help people and businesses communicate effortlessly. We make communication easier, faster and more reliable for customers, while delivering value to our stakeholders' and its *Goals*, which are: 'To create sustainable long-term growth, to deliver superior returns to shareholders and positive impact to stakeholders'. The commitment to doing the right thing by the environment and at the same time running a thriving business – clearly informs the Purpose behind Singtel's approach to sustainability. The addition of an actual, overarching Purpose statement would be a great one. As Graham Kenny, the CEO of strategic consultancy firm Strategic Factors says in a *Harvard Business Review* article (September 2014) entitled: "Your Company's Purpose is not its Mission, Vision or Values":

> *If you're crafting a purpose statement, my advice is this: To inspire your staff to do good work for you, find a way to express the organisation's impact on the lives of customers, clients, students, patients – whomever you're trying to serve. Make them feel it.*

He goes on to cite the following companies as good examples of Purpose-driven firms: financial services company ING ('Empowering people to stay a step ahead in life and in business'; the Kellogg food company ('Nourishing families so that they can flourish and thrive') and the insurance company IAG ('To help people manage risk and recover from the hardship of unexpected loss'). What all these have in common is that they try to capture the human element in their Purpose and the impact the company wants to have on *people*. The other thing they have in common is that they are all solid answers to the question: *Why are we here doing what we're doing?* If you work in a company or organisation that cannot answer this question, I suggest you'll eventually start to encounter problems (probably sooner rather than later). If your employer can't articulate their organisational purpose satisfactorily, that is, in a frank and authentic way – the whole Purpose + MVV (Mission, Vision, Values) combination will start to ring hollow. And if your employer starts to behave or act in a way that conflicts with the declared Purpose + MVV, that's when you will begin to feel uneasy and uncomfortable. We have seen this with the employees of companies like Facebook and Google: people joined these companies with aspirations to do good in the world. When the company fails to live out its values in the way its employees expect it to behave – it is a dangerous situation to be in. Engagement levels and employee net promotor scores tend to take a tumble if such companies are found not to be practising what they preach. And if anything, the generation of employees today that grew up as digital natives with high ethical standards – are unforgiving and brutal in their judgement once made. Jeff Fromm (CMO Network) and an expert on Millennials, Generation Z and the impact of purpose and sustainability, states in an article in *Forbes* (16 January 2019):

> *Purpose isn't profitable when it's disingenuous. It has to be real. In this age of digital transparency customers can see through it and will redirect their spend elsewhere.*

Jeff goes on to mention Unilever as a good example where its 'Sustainable Living' brands – which include Knorr, Dove and Lipton – are growing 50% faster than the company's other brands and account for more than 60% of Unilever's growth, thereby showing that it is certainly possible to balance Purpose *with* Profit.

We have taken a look at Purpose in a work context. The evidence shows that people who work for organisations with a purpose that they believe and buy-into – will stay longer, be happier and perform better. Glassdoor data in 2020 for Unilever shows (UK data) a rating of four stars out of five with 86% of employees saying that they would recommend the company to a friend (the Glassdoor average is 56%).

We can also see that organisations that link their Purpose to sustainability and who can prove that they are genuine in doing this – stand to benefit more than those who don't. Examples of such companies include Nike. Here's their Purpose statement:

Purpose Moves Us.

Our purpose is to unite the world through sport to create a healthy planet, active communities and an equal playing field for all.

HOW CAN PURPOSE BE STRENGTHENED? WHERE DO EXPERT HUMANS COME IN?

In their article published in October 2019 'Purpose is Everything', a team from Deloitte outlined the case for Purpose-driven companies. They took the opportunity to describe Purpose-driven strategy in a clear and unequivocal way by using their own company as an example:

> **Put all humans at the heart of your decisions** ... *at Deloitte, our purpose – making an impact that matters – serves as the soil from which everything else grows, influencing and fuelling life in all parts of our organization, work and talent. Our purpose guides everything that we do ....*

Thinkers and advocates for putting Purpose forward as the most fundamental organisational principle include Carol Cone, Founder of the Purpose Collective, who has been working on and advocating for Purpose since the 1980s. In her 2019 article for Salesforce.org, 'What does a Purpose-driven Company look like?', Carol itemises the following key aspects:

Purpose-driven companies:

1. Integrate purpose into core business strategy.

2. Link employees' day-to-day work to a larger shared purpose.

3. Use a purpose mindset to advance measurable goals.

4. Harness the power of purpose to innovate.

5. Engage their partners around purpose.

6. Know what they stand for.

Likewise, the HR thinker and author Josh Bersin in his 2015 work on employee engagement identified five key areas which would need attention if employee engagement were to thrive. Under 'Meaningful work', one of the items included 'Autonomy', as identified by Dan Pink in *Drive*. Under 'Hands-on Management', Josh includes 'coaching and investment in management development'. Under 'Positive work environment', he mentions 'Humanistic workplace'. Under 'Growth Opportunity' he lists 'Training and support on the job'. And last but not least, he includes 'Trust in Leadership', which is where 'Mission and Purpose' appear. The work, in which these key areas appear – 'Becoming Irresistible – A New Model for Employee Engagement' – represents a major step forward. And I think *Expert Humans* can build on this good work, that of Carol Cone, and others.

EXPERT HUMANS – HOW THE ACE MODEL OF ALTRUISM, COMPASSION AND EMPATHY CAN SUPPORT PURPOSE

We will be taking a deeper dive into what really constitutes altruism, compassion, and empathy in Chapter 5 – *Breaking New Ground*. But for now let us consider how these three things affect Purpose and ask: if we apply them, how do they support and advance Purpose?

The literature on Purpose, Mission, Vision, and Values is littered with references to companies spending time and money on trying to define what all these things might be for their organisations. They do this work through workshops and pan-organisational initiatives to 'surface' stuff. As we have seen, some companies and organisations do achieve break-through success with this work – if the work from the outset is characterised by authenticity and truth and if the process is well-thought through and the facilitation supportive and challenging. But too often, these initiatives can fall victim to a classic tick-box mentality and once the values, for example, are agreed upon, after hours of word-smithing and debate (and dispute), a nice-sounding acronym is born and with astonishing speed, starts turning up on websites, in 'on-boarding' documentation for new arrivals into the company – and perhaps even nicely framed and hung up in the reception area or boardroom. Job done.

But of course it's not a case of 'job done'. Such work cannot be done in a meaningful way unless the culture of the organisation is being attended to at the same time. Words like 'integrity' and 'customer-centricity' are, as we all know, all well and good – but without a real sense of what these things mean in the context of the culture of that particular organisation, we are only ever going to get a feeble version of what could be possible.

This is where creating the 'Humanistic Workplace' that Josh Bersin mentioned – becomes critical. What does that look like in reality? The 'Humanistic Workplace' is a great start but it needs to evolve and be defined in ways that people in organisations can understand and say: 'Yeah, I'll buy into that. That sounds like something I'd like to see'.

In the early 2000s, I remember a friend telling me that her boss told her that she never missed a direct report's birthday and would always send (via her long-suffering PA) or hand-deliver a card to that person herself. She had even detailed her PA to make a spreadsheet with everyone's name on it, their birth-date, the name of their significant 'other' and a note about whether they had any children – and what their names were. She told my friend that she should do the same. This was because her boss thought it important that employees know that 'we cared for them'. In another company, I heard about a CEO who liked to spend most of his time ensconced in his office, enjoying the beautiful views of the countryside, seldom venturing out and having sandwiches delivered to his desk every day. Yet he was adamant that it was also necessary to 'walk the corridors' to 'pulse-check' the workforce and 'keep an ear to the ground'. So he would walk the corridors. At the same time, every week – at 4.30pm to be precise. People told me that this was done on such a regular basis that they could set their watches for the moment when he would put his head round the door and ask cheerily: 'Everyone doing OK? Yes? Great!' before disappearing. By 5pm, he had jumped into his car and was homeward bound.

Clearly different people have different notions about what constitutes a 'Humanistic Workplace.' A birthday card once a year and a weekly check-in is not going to cut it. The problem is that authenticity is lacking and if that's the case, then fine words about Purpose are likely to fall on deaf ears. In contrast to this approach though, companies that have started the journey towards building more compassionate workplaces are much more likely to see Purpose thrive: this is because Purpose is the foundation for everything and in an environment characterised by warmth and humanity, by compassion and empathy, Purpose has true meaning.

And, as we will examine shortly, altruism also has a key role to play in strengthening and being strengthened by Purpose.

But first let's take a look at altruism and sustainability.

HOW CAN LEADERS AND MANAGERS USE AN EXPERT HUMANS MINDSET (OF ALTRUISM, COMPASSION AND EMPATHY) TO ADVANCE THE SUSTAINABILITY AGENDA – WHAT DOES SUCH A MINDSET LOOK LIKE?

'I don't want you to be hopeful. I want you to panic … I want you to feel the fear I feel every day … And then I want you to act'.

Greta Thunberg speaking at the World Economic Forum in Davos, 2019.

This book is about disruption of various kinds and looks at what kind of new leadership is needed to deal with our disrupted world. Greta Thunberg has told us that 'our house is on fire' and although she may not be everyone's favourite person, her words are clear and unequivocal. We are being disrupted by climate change and the signs are that things are going to get worse. Depending on your own view and where you sit on the political spectrum, you might be gravely pessimistic, or you might think that this is something that's serious but not something you can do anything about. I'm going to assume that it is something that you *are* concerned about because I'd like to bring up the topic of altruism – which I think still has a tendency to be overlooked, even as its cousins Compassion and Empathy start to get more airtime (when the topics of leadership and organisational development are being discussed). We will look at the historical and psychological background to altruism in Chapters 5 and 6 but for now let's reflect on what, if any, contribution altruism has to play in the context of sustainability.

In its *Greater Good* magazine, the Greater Good Science Center at UC Berkeley has this definition of altruism:

Altruism is when we act to promote someone else's welfare, even at a risk or cost to ourselves. Though some believe that humans are fundamentally self-interested, recent research suggests otherwise: studies have found that people's first impulse is to cooperate rather than compete; that toddlers spontaneously help people in need out of a genuine concern for their welfare; and that even non-human primates display altruism.

When it comes to *corporate* altruism, most people are familiar with the areas of philanthropy and Corporate Social Responsibility (CSR) – where companies give financial and other forms of support to individuals and communities, without a declared expectation of direct benefit to the companies themselves. These can range from the support that a local large employer gives to the community, or specific sections of a given local community, usually in the form of staff time and sometimes in the form of cash donations. It is well-recognised that such 'corporate altruism' is good for employees as they sign up to volunteer in a variety of settings. And as we will discover more when we look at what happens to our brain chemistry in Chapter 5, doing good feels good and does us good. Then there is corporate giving on a monumental scale where gigantic global multinationals or their foundations, dig deep to fund initiatives of many kinds, designed to improve the lives of people all over the world. Examples include the Bill and Melinda Gates Foundation, the largest private foundation of its kind in the world with more than $46.8 billion in assets.

So there is really no shortage of 'corporate altruism', it would seem. That said, we will look at just how altruistic 'corporate altruism' is in Chapter 6 – 'Altruism in the Workplace.'

What we need to ponder, therefore, is whether there is a way to encourage more individual altruism – as we see in smaller community-based initiatives – among a broader population still. In times of disruption, we feel good when we hear stories of individual heroism and selflessness. Is there a way to capture this essence, so that what we learn and experience during times of turbulence, we can deploy at other, less extreme times? We looked at how disruption on a global scale occurs in peaks and troughs and we know that there are very few so-called Black Swan events (catastrophic events which are impossible to predict). Pandemics for example are not Black Swan events. Pandemics happen (and will continue to happen). The real test of such events for humanity is the degree to which we are prepared for them (or not).

Encouraging people to be *more* altruistic – to do good without the promise of any discernible, personal benefit – might seem unrealistic and idealistic. But there has never been a better time to try:

- '[…] younger generations … want to work at companies with an authentic purpose, with more than 70 percent of millennials expecting their employers to focus on societal or mission-driven problems'. (Deloitte Insights)

- Digital transformation has connected the world in ways that could hardly have been imagined even a short while ago. The possibility for the world to feel connected as one, is still possible.

- There is an incentive to encourage people to try to be Expert Humans – people who are altruistic, compassionate and empathic. The world of work is changing and the humanising of it is underway.

- Humanising the workplace is one way to change the world for the better.

- There is a strong argument, above and beyond the notion of doing well and doing good, that when it comes to sustainability, companies and their employees should strive to do things right – without personal gain. As the American cultural anthropologist Margaret Mead (1901–1978) famously noted: 'We won't have a society if we destroy the environment'.

If the items listed above are to be realistic goals, we will need to champion a new kind of leadership. This is where Expert Human leaders have a critical role to play.

3

IMPACT – WHAT IMPACT WILL THIS DISRUPTION HAVE ON HUMANS AND THE WORKPLACE?

- What will happen if we do not change?
- What benefits will accrue if we do change?
- Implications for mental health and general wellbeing: new organisational cultures.
- Why a change is needed now

WHAT WILL HAPPEN IF WE DO NOT CHANGE?

Change at The Macro-level

Change at the global or macro-level will have to happen in a number of critical areas, chief among them being political, social, economic, environmental – and what we might broadly term global human health. Clearly, the extent to which any of these variables can be altered will affect the nature, degree, and intensity of the impact on humanity. We will take a look at change and impact at the micro-level – and at the workplace level – in a short while. But for now let's focus on what is happening now and what might happen in the decade to come.

Table 2: Macrotrends Emerging over the Next Decade According to the World Business Council for Sustainable Development and Adapted by the Author.

Demographics	Environment	Economy
Generational leadership handover	Worsening climate impacts, pervasive global health concerns	Short-term crisis, long-term slow down
Population growth in Asia and Africa	Local pollution, degradation and scarcity create demand for innovation	Peak globalisation and the rise of Asia
Technology	**Politics**	**Culture**
Automation impacts every industry and country	Polarisation and radicalism on the rise	Post-materialism: attitudes and lifestyles diverge
Datafication (leading to massive productivity gains but more surveillance)	Geopolitical instability (weakened multilateralism)	Culture wars escalate (young–old, urban–rural, rich–poor)

Table 2 is based on an analysis by the World Business Council for Sustainable Development (WBCSD) and provides a useful snapshot of the macrotrends emerging over the next decade. Even a cursory glance at this list of issues should be sufficient to fill any reader with a mixture of fear, concern and perhaps even hopelessness. What to do? What to do *first*?

Some argue that there should be a rank order or prioritisation of the challenges we face. For example, if we aren't able to manage a global health crisis effectively, we run the real risk of seeing a collapse in the economic order, with knock-on effects into the world of politics and a real danger of social unrest as an outcome of the failure of the whole set of elements to come together. In its 4 July 2020 issue, one of *The Economist*'s main stories was about the COVID-19 pandemic – 'The Way We Live Now – how COVID-19 is yet to do its worst'. It referenced a Massachusetts Institute of Technology research study of 84 countries which painted a truly bleak picture of what might be to come. The key points:

- By spring 2021, between 1.4 million and 3.7 million people would have lost their lives.

- Well over 90% of the world's population would still be vulnerable to infection – especially if immunity were to turn out to be transient.

These numbers are difficult for human beings to process. More Americans have lost their lives than were lost in the Vietnam War. Minority communities across the world have been hardest hit and the scale of human loss is truly monumental. In addition to this, prioritisation of effort against the range of problems facing us presents moral and ethical problems on a global scale which quickly translate into political issues at the national and even local level. When asked whether the #1 priority is public health or the economy, some politicians are quick and firm in their response: it has to be about the people. Others are not so sure, especially when it happens to be a big election year when people (in most countries) vote based on their assessment of what the economy is doing, that is, do I have a job? Can I put bread on the table?

So it may be that COVID-19 is here to stay, in one form or another. And it is highly likely that we will need to deal with new and possibly even more deadly pandemics. How ready are we? One thing we do know is that encroachment by people on the habitats of wild animals is increasing the possibility of zoonotic diseases jumping from animals to humans. Examples of these diseases include Ebola, West Nile virus, and SARS. They all started in animals and made the transition into humans. This seems a hard fact to dispute. A BBC report from July 2020 quoting UN experts says:

Zoonotic diseases ... are increasing and will continue to do so without action to protect wildlife and preserve the environment.

The experts attribute the rise in diseases such as COVID-19 to high demand for animal protein, unsustainable agricultural practices and climate change. They estimate that neglected zoonotic diseases kill two million people a year. The economic cost is also stupendous: COVID-19 is set to cost the global economy $49 trillion over two years (BBC News, 7 July 2020).

It is hard to think of any quick fixes that we could deploy to mitigate this danger. That's probably because there aren't any.

And there are other effects of the pandemic that concern businesses, namely a growing trend towards 'cutting corners' and relaxing erstwhile laws protecting the environment in order to help kick-start economies. Stephen Olson is a Research Fellow at the Hinrich Foundation (which is concerned with the advancement of sustainable global trade) and he has over 30 years of international trade experience, including time as an international trade negotiator in Washington, DC, serving on the US negotiating team for

NAFTA negotiations. As Stephen points out in his article 'Will COVID-19 advance sustainable trade?':

> *Indonesia … is back-tracking on efforts to curtail rampant illegal logging. Exporters are no longer required to obtain licenses verifying that their timber and finished wood products come from legal sources. These licenses had helped reassure importers that their Indonesian timber purchases were being harvested in sustainable ways.*

There are signs that the pressure to breathe new life into failing local economies is also eroding employment practices:

> *In India, for example, several states including Uttar Pradesh, Madhya Pradesh, Rajasthan and Gujarat have amended legislation to provide labour law exemptions on issues including working hours and safety inspections. These exemptions apply both to existing businesses and new businesses being established, presumably as an added inducement to set up facilities in India. (Olson, 2020)*

'OUR HOUSE IS ON FIRE'

As mentioned earlier, Greta Thunberg said in one of her speeches: 'Our house is on fire'. This observation has resonated strongly with me, as has her assertion that if the world is able to mobilise as it has tried to do with respect to containing or eliminating coronavirus, why can it not mobilise to tackle what many people believe is a *truly* existential crisis? There are many reasons why this has not happened (yet): it seems that until we witness even more extreme examples of climate change happening *in the major urban areas of the world,* politicians and governments won't really take notice and act. And as many climate change campaigners have warned, time and again, it will be too late by then. We know from studies of empathy that human beings find it hard to truly empathise with the suffering of others if those others are literally thousands of miles away from us and are not 'like us'. We tend to be able to do empathy better when horror, disaster and catastrophe are closer to home. Right on our doorstep. (We will take a deeper dive into the question of bias in empathy in Chapter 8). The problem, as we all know, is that our world is inextricably linked in so many ways that we have to tackle environmental issues at both a macro- and a micro-level – at the global level as well as at the local level. We can do the best we can in our local areas and communities from paying attention to how we recycle to how we protect the wildlife in our sphere of influence. This is fantastic stuff, but we know that on its own, it won't be enough to bring about sustainable change.

But there's still lots that can and should be done at the *micro-level* which, done right, can effect change at the macro-level. We will look at that in just a moment.

Before we do so, we should recognise that there are a plethora of *other* issues apart from pandemics and climate change that we need to think about as we consider the future of the planet. One of the biggest and most insidious is the question of inequality. This is one of the major disruptors of all time, given that it undermines and destroys the possibility that as a species, we can have everyone achieve their true potential, realise their dreams, and fulfil their aspirations. It is also something that connects directly to some of the other big issues that we have to face. For developing economies, it is well-recognised that the greatest determinant of societal advancement is women's emancipation and education. This is key to the creation of peaceful environments in which children can develop and grow, where businesses can flourish and where everyone can enjoy a better quality of life.

An African proverb says:

> *If you educate a man, you educate an individual. But if you educate a woman, you educate a nation.*

And Michelle Obama is quoted as saying:

> *When girls are educated, their countries become stronger and more prosperous.*

We also know that people from minorities across the developed and developing world have to struggle in ways that more advantaged people find it hard to fully 'get'. There is what we might term an 'Empathy Deficit'. The Black Lives Matter movement has made some significant progress in shining a light on the plight of black people in the United States and further afield, to be sure: and at the same time, we appreciate that there is still an awfully long way to go. Progress has been made in countries like Australia and

New Zealand to build a better and fairer society for their indigenous peoples – and it will be great to see what further progress can be made in the years to come. We also know that there are many countries around the world where racial hatred and minority suppression is endemic. These situations appear as great monoliths, supremely resistant to change: to bring more humanity to the people in these countries is a gargantuan task where the changes needed and the time required to achieve change – are likely to be countable only in generations, not even years. Old enmities are hard to overcome as history shows. Our task is to ensure that we don't just add to these enmities and stoke the fires of hatred. We can do this by advocating strongly for a different way of being and behaving. And what better place to start than in our own backyards, wherever we may be, in our places of work and in our homes (which is in fact the same place for many people now!)

The chipping away at the monoliths can start right here, right now.

CHANGE AT THE MICRO-LEVEL

For our purposes – and to make this a practical, actionable activity – let's look at *change at the micro-level* from the perspective of the workplace. Our working hypothesis in *Expert Humans*, put simply, is to imagine what the workplace would need to look like if we were to make it more human: and our intention – in making it more human – is to enable the achievement of a broad set of objectives:

- To enable people to enjoy being at work.

- To reduce stress and burnout and improve mental health at work.

- To foster stronger bonds between co-workers.

- To create psychological safety.

- To establish a climate of innovation and creativity.

- To enable people to handle change and disruption *and critically*

- To help support the sustainability agenda through better leadership.

If we could begin to address these things, I believe it would be a great start. But just as we rush to get going, we need to recognise a few things.

First: what do we mean by 'the workplace'? The concept of the office is being disrupted by digital transformation and global pandemics. 'Going to the office' might just become a thing of the past. Second: it's worth noting that there are workers who never go to an office. Freelancers and sole proprietors, entrepreneurs and gig-workers riding deliveries – the formal, traditional office isn't a 'thing' for them. Nor is it a thing for the vast communities of carers around the world – people doing a day's work just like anyone else, caring for a loved one in the home – well, they just don't identify with the construct. Third: we learned through COVID-19 about the unsung s(h)eroes represented by the 'essential' frontline workers – those in hospitals working alongside fantastic medical staff; cleaners working at transport hubs and cleaning and serving staff in canteens and other vital eating venues, baristas and shop assistants – none of these people are to be found in offices. Fourth: online communication and a vast array of tools to keep us connected mean that the need for something like an office as a meeting place for humans – is being profoundly challenged. Fifth: do we understand the potential economic damage that we will need to manage as a collateral effect of the demise of the traditional office, as the numbers of coffee shops and sandwich bars dwindle in line with the reduction in numbers of urban office workers? Or will we see it as a positive, given that fewer people will need to commute (good for the environment and good for minimising social contact in the era of the pandemic)? Sixth: what are the implications for our plans to humanise the workplace, if over time, 'humans in offices' go the way of the dinosaurs? Will they?

The traditional workplace – disappearing? There are signs that the big companies are moving fast to reduce the number of employees present in offices. Twitter was one of the first to report the change (in May 2020) and in July 2020, in an announcement that was highly significant, given that it came from the Japanese technology firm Fujitsu, the company said that its 'Work Life Shift' programme would introduce a hitherto unseen level of flexibility for its 80,000 workers in Japan. Working from home would be deemed standard practice. Such changes are significant anywhere in the world, but for it to be gaining pace in Japan, the land of the salaried, white-collar worker, this marks a real shift. Japan observers sometimes remark that as a society, Japan is often resistant to change – changing only as a result of what the Japanese call '*gaiatsu*' or 'external pressure'. While some might say that this is a bit of an exaggeration, we could see the arrival of COVID-19 as a pivotal moment for Japan (as for many countries) where an external force arrived suddenly and with little warning. Pressure to change came more or less immediately.

Working from home (WFH) – the pandemic has hastened the 'normalisation' of 'WFH'. It has also given rise to a new type of anxiety around mental wellbeing – amidst concerns that people find it challenging to work from home (due to children and pets demanding attention) or they keep on working at the expense of any kind of downtime, raising the spectre of burnout. Other people are more sanguine about these matters, saying that they like the flexibility that WFH offers and would prefer not to have to waste time commuting. Whatever the true picture I think it is still early in the evolution of mass-scale WFH to be able to fully assess the impact on human beings. What, for example, is the longer-term effect of not being able to have water-cooler conversations? Can these really be fully substituted for, in a digital sense? We will return to this topic later in the book.

Non-office-based workers – for people working for hail-ride and delivery companies, transportation firms, and airlines, the 'workplace' is a multifarious thing. For restaurant and bar staff, café and teahouse owners and workers – they certainly have a physical space in which they carry out their work. And the carers I just mentioned feel passionate about the fact that they are working, just like everybody else – but that their workplace is in fact their loved-one's home. Workers in care homes are another group of largely 'taken-for-granted-people' who have a clearly defined 'workplace' which isn't an office.

So for our purposes let's regard the 'workplace' as a 'thing' rather than a physical space. That way we can talk about relationships in the workplace to mean, broadly, 'the relationships we have with people when we are at work'.

(In this connection, it was interesting for me to hear that, despite all the flexibility and independence of being an Uber driver and all the technological apparatus inherent in that job, when an Uber driver is feeling low and needs someone to talk to, they don't need to interact with a chatbot. An actual human being is on hand to help out.)

Supporting the sustainability agenda through better leadership – there's a felt sense among leadership and organisational development experts – one that is shared by sustainability advocates – that even as we see an increasing number of companies producing data about their green credentials and their green initiatives, we are still not seeing the kind of mindset shift from the top that will be necessary if business (specifically) is to make the critical contribution required to shift things. In Germany, there is a feeling that 'first tier' managers, that is, not the C-level executives – do exhibit an open-mindedness that is going to be important if the sustainability agenda is to be embraced. There's an idea that these younger managers are the ones who hold the keys to future success. Help them to get clear on sustainability, give them the data to support their arguments, and enable them to make their points to upper management – if we could do this then we would see the emergence of a class of sustainability champions able to convince the C-level to go further and do more.

By adding altruism, compassion, and empathy into the leadership development mix, there's a great chance we could get some of the change that we need if we are to succeed in our sustainability efforts.

WHAT BENEFITS WILL ACCRUE IF WE DO CHANGE?

Benefits at The Macro-level

One of the most immediate and obvious effects of the COVID-19 pandemic was to reduce the number of vehicles on roads across the globe and curtail mass transport and air travel. There were aerial 'before and after' photographs of Beijing and other major conurbations like Delhi which showed brown, grainy cityscapes replaced by pictures of soaring blue skies. It showed us all what might be possible if pollution levels could be drastically reduced. At the same time, many observers noted ruefully that the moment lockdowns were relaxed, and people got back on the roads and back in the air, it would be no time at all before we would be back to pre-COVID-19 levels of pollution. Marine park officials in Thailand reported sightings of sea creatures coming close to shore that no one could remember seeing in such large numbers before. They attributed this to the sudden drop in visitors to the Thai island marine reserves and the reduction in small motorboat activity taking tourists to various islands, shoals, and sandbanks. The officials also noticed a new 'blue-ness' in the colour of the ocean. Across the world from North Wales to Canadian prairie towns there were reports of all kinds of animals venturing into urban areas, emboldened by the lack of humans on the streets due to the lockdowns in place. As a BBC report in March 2020 noted:

> *A herd of goats has taken over a deserted town centre, eating hedges and flowers from gardens. Usually the wild herd of about 122 Kashmiri goats venture into Llandudno during bad weather. Town councillor Carol Marubbi believes the lack of people around because of coronavirus has drawn them in. She said everyone in Llandudno was 'very proud of the animals' and that they had been providing 'free' entertainment to people watching from their windows.*

Such endearing stories are great to read but they are in relatively short supply compared with seemingly endless reports about the devastation of the animal world. These continue apace.

WORKING TO RAISE AWARENESS

As we know, there are many great organisations striving tirelessly to raise awareness about climate change and protection of the environment. One such organisation working alongside business in order to bring about change – is the WBCSD (The World Business Council for Sustainable Development). The WBCSD is active on many different fronts, partnering with various like-minded organisations to look for practical and pragmatic ways to support and advance the sustainability agenda. An encouraging initiative that caught my eye was announced in New York in September 2019 – a joint endeavour by WBCSD and the Nature4Climate coalition called 'Natural climate solutions: the business perspective', which is a guide to finding natural climate solutions for the private sector. In it, Maria Mendiluce, Managing Director of the WBCSD, says:

> *We are entering a period of transformation from where we are today to a low-carbon economy and a sustainable land sector. Nature provides a solution for both; it can capture and sequester carbon while producing food, protecting biodiversity, and sustaining life. Responsible investment and supportive policy will help us to scale up natural climate solutions, providing one-third of the emissions reductions we need to meet the Paris Agreement targets by 2030.*

The WBCSD goes on to mention studies indicating that natural climate solutions could indeed provide around 30% of the emissions reductions needed if we are to meet the Paris Agreement for targets for 2030. These efforts must surely be welcomed as a great addition to the activities currently being undertaken by businesses across the world to do what they can do to mitigate damage to the environment and to tackle climate change. That said, it is clear that things are not moving as quickly and with the sense of urgency felt by climate change activists, nor with anything like the speed at which we should be doing things, as pointed out by scientists around the world. And at the same time, there has to be some cause for optimism. If we are to see benefits at the macro-level, I believe it will come as a result of a different kind of leadership. This is where the macro-level and the micro-level converge.

EMERGENCE OF A NEW KIND OF LEADERSHIP FOR A DISRUPTED WORLD – ADVANCING SUSTAINABILITY AND HUMANITY

There is some excellent work going on around the world to try to identify what we might mean by 'a new kind of leadership' for the world we are living in now and the one we will occupy in the future. Monika Kolb of the M3TRIX Academy in Germany, which concerns itself with guiding sustainable business transformation, believes that we need younger leaders at the middle manager level in organisations to be developed in a way that not only helps them to integrate sustainability into the core business and along the entire value chain – but also helps to develop them as sustainability champions, able to influence the C-level while also preparing them, as younger managers, for future senior leadership roles. Monika's work combines sustainable management, business transformation and responsible leadership. It also brings in a focus on the manager as human being – and as such the themes of altruism, compassion and empathy resonate strongly for her.

As an example of how sustainable business works in practice, Table 3 shows how Kimberly–Clark achieves sustainable action throughout its value chain and product life cycle. It's interesting to note the important human references – such as human rights and ethical practices and social compliance audits in the supplier manufacturing stage of the cycle.

Table 3:   Sustainability Throughout the Kimberly–Clark Value Chain (from 2019 Global Kimberly–Clark Sustainability Report, Adapted by the Author).

Stage of the Product Life Cycle	Sustainable Development Goals Addressed	Impacts and Opportunities
Raw materials	1, 13, 15 (No poverty; climate action; life on land)	Forest-dependent communities; forest carbon footprint; biodiversity
Supplier manufacturing	6, 8, 13 (Clean water and sanitation; decent work and economic growth; climate action)	Sustainable water use; water stewardship; human rights and ethical practices; social compliance audits; Scope 3 emissions
Kimberly–Clark manufacturing	6, 12, 13 (Clean water; responsible production and consumption; climate action)	Sustainable water use; water stewardship; zero waste to landfill; Scope 1 & 2 emissions
Distribution	13 (Climate action)	Scope 3 emissions
Customers	3, 13 (Good health and wellbeing; climate action)	Improving access; Scope 3 emissions
Consumers	3, 5, 6 (Good health and wellbeing; climate action)	Health and wellbeing of people; progress of women and ending stigmas; access to clean water and sanitation
Product end of life (to recovery or to residual waste)	13 (Climate action)	Post-consumer waste

As Table 3 indicates, there is also a reference to the work that Kimberly–Clark does to de-stigmatise menstruation – a huge issue for women in a number of developing nations ('Progress of women and ending stigmas').

There is no doubt that there is an exceptionally strong *Do Well and Do Good* ethos running throughout this major global company.

And in 2019, the UK-based Corporate Research Forum published a thoroughly detailed and valuable report by Professor David Grayson OBE and Dr Carmen von Rohr called *Responsible Business: How can HR drive the agenda?* In the report, Professor Grayson and his colleagues list five individual qualities associated with strong responsible leadership, under the following rubrics: Purpose (possessing a strong purpose and values set), Plan (understanding the context of sustainable development trends), Culture (showing humility, authenticity and with a clear communication style), Collaboration (ability to conceive and conceptualise how collaborations with other businesses and parts of society might work, and to end such collaborations too, if necessary) plus Advocacy (responsible leaders are politically aware and adept at using social media. Importantly, they also possess the kind of networking skills needed to foster systemic change).

I think this is a useful contribution to the debate about what critical leadership skills are needed in a disrupted world and is something that we can add to and build on. We will explore in the coming chapters how altruism, compassion, and empathy can be brought in to strengthen such core responsible leadership attributes as shared by scholars and practitioners like Professor Grayson, Dr von Rohr and Monika Kolb.

IMPLICATIONS FOR MENTAL HEALTH AND GENERAL WELLBEING

In the next section of the book – Part Two (Chapter 4) – we will be looking in some detail at the foundational aspects of human psychology insofar as it shapes and affects altruism, compassion and empathy in organisational life. Before we move on to that, let's take a look at the current state of mental health in the workplace through the following 'impact lenses':

Impact Lens #1   *Digital Transformation*

Deloitte published a report in 2019 entitled *Leading the Social Enterprise – Reinvent with a Human Focus*. The report featured data for the world ('Global') and for Southeast Asia ('SEA'). The respondents to the Deloitte survey underpinning the report – were only too aware of the tremendous disruption making its way towards them. And the key finding was that rather than replacing humans, what we can expect is to see humans and bots increasingly working 'side-by-side'.

The other finding (which might not come as a surprise to everyone) was that people felt that the state of readiness of firms to deal effectively with digital change and transformation – was low.

In my experience looking at the effect of digital disruption, there is no doubt that the issue is a human one, not a technical one. There seems to be broad agreement that this is the case. The impact from AI in virtually every sphere of the workplace is likely to be ongoing and its effect on humans and their mental health is not only apparent – but set to move in directions that few would have been able to predict.

CO-EXISTENCE OF HUMANS WITH AI

One example of the co-existence of humans with AI involves bots in the banking industry. Anyone today who wants to interact with their bank is likely to encounter bots taking care of less complex and more mundane enquiries, with frequent exhortations to check out the bank's website for the answer they seek. From a user perspective, such interactions are not particularly sophisticated and for anything out of the ordinary, the name of the game is to try your best to chase down a human if at all possible. Not easy as anyone who has attempted to discover where a missing internet transfer has disappeared to, will know. I have heard from developers of banking bots that an interesting and not entirely foreseen outcome of the advance of the bots, comes from frontline banking executives reporting a sense of loss in terms of empathy and empathic conversations with the client that they were always used to – given the role in early interaction with the customer when they first call in is now largely played by bots. This phenomenon may well be overstated and perhaps many bank employees are more than happy for the bots to occupy the front line (especially when it comes to dealing with irate customers). And then there are customers who report that they are more than happy to interact with a bot and dispense with any of the niceties of old-style 'banter'. Nevertheless there is this sense that bots can come between humans – and some people don't like that. In later chapters, we will return to this topic of AI and its impact on the mental state of humans.

Impact Lens #2   *Sustainability*

It goes without saying that sustainability and the question of general human wellbeing are inextricably linked. Nowhere is this perhaps more obvious than in the context of what we eat and drink – and it is clear that water security is a top concern for the majority of countries around the world. A real concern now – which will only get worse over time – is the future of the great rivers of the world. The geopolitical, economic, and environmental impacts of decisions taken by some nation states – which might not have been made in everyone's interests – are set to have extremely far-reaching consequences. The construction of Ethiopia's Nile River dam is one such example which involves Ethiopia, Sudan, and Egypt in challenging discussions. Another is the Mekong in South East Asia, a huge concern for the countries of Laos, Cambodia, and Vietnam. As David Hutt reported in the *Asia Times* (October 2019) 'Water War Risk Rising on the Mekong':

China now has the power to completely stop the flow of water to downstream nations, a pressure point that could be used to devastate their agricultural economies and create food scarcity in the event of a conflict.

This is an example of where altruism, compassion and empathy are entirely absent – victim on a global scale to geopolitical leveraging and power politics, some would say.

Impact Lens #3   *Global health challenges and pandemics*

It seems clear that we can expect ongoing shocks and increasing mental stress for people struggling to survive in the COVID era. S&P Global Market Intelligence shared alarming headlines during the summer of 2020:

> **Unprecedented consumer collapse stokes fear for future of US economy**
>
> *The American consumer may never be the same.*
>
> *Facing the most severe economic shock in a century, they are saving more than ever while spending has fallen off a cliff. While those extremes are unlikely to last, the trauma of mass unemployment, lower wages and economic insecurity could leave scars that permanently change the behavior of those responsible for more than two-thirds of the US economy.*
> *(Brian Scheid, S&P, Macroeconomics)*

Sobering words.

NEW ORGANISATIONAL CULTURES AND WHY A CHANGE IS NEEDED NOW

The disruptors of our times are many: our environment is under threat; our way of life is being altered almost on a daily basis by global health catastrophes; our way of working is being transformed by digital transformation on many fronts; widespread inequalities persist and our political and economic systems are being assaulted from all directions. It is hardly surprising that the way we organise, manage, and lead ourselves is being scrutinised and questioned like never before.

We will look at organisational culture change in more detail in the chapters to come but for now, I think we can be sure that significant change is in the air.

This is why a change in the way we do things round here – is long overdue. And one obvious starting point is to look at ourselves. What will it take to make us Expert Humans?

PART TWO

HOW DO WE FIT IN?

4

DRAWING ON HUMAN PSYCHOLOGY

- How can we draw on human psychology to help us make sense of this emerging world of disharmony and unpredictability?

- What 'hidden gems' exist in our human experience such that we can magnify and deploy them for our own good and the wellbeing and resilience of others?

- The emergent and critical aspect of psychological safety at work.

- Attachment theory and safe spaces – how these ideas relate to 'good' work and how we can learn to develop ourselves to be instruments for the creation of such spaces ('Use of Self').

HOW CAN WE DRAW ON HUMAN PSYCHOLOGY TO HELP US MAKE SENSE OF THIS EMERGING WORLD OF DISHARMONY AND UNPREDICTABILITY?

As we have explored in the previous three chapters of *Expert Humans*, we are living in a time of increasing disharmony, unpredictability, and disruption exacerbated by the sheer pace and scale of all the dislocation and turbulence. The world has experienced tremendous change before – with many tumultuous events taking place during a single lifetime. I am thinking here of the Second World War and the falling of the Iron Curtain as examples: so as a species we are certainly not newcomers to mayhem, chaos, and tumult.

What has been will be again, what has been done will be done
again, there is nothing new under the sun.

(From the Book of Solomon)

While these words allow us some reflection and even some cause for com-fort, the facts as they appear before us signal that we are on a path to a truly existential crisis for civilisation and the world, unless we course-correct. The disruptors to our way of life are clear. What is not so clear is the exact shape that these disruptors will take or what the change – or damage they could inflict – will turn out to be. The best course of action is to be prepared – and that includes being prepared psychologically for the ruptures that will with-out doubt, continue. So – far from being defeatist and pessimistic – I think we need to do what we can to embrace the changes that are coming our way and get ourselves into as good a shape mentally as we possibly can.

So what would that entail?

Well, we have considered previously how the world looks at the moment, as well as what looks to be coming our way in the coming decade, at both the macro- and the micro-level. We know that our political leaders, some more than others, are in a position where they are ready, willing, and able to effect changes at a grand scale affecting millions of people. That's pretty clear. In some countries, we can reject political leaders at the ballot box whereas in other countries we know that that is not so straightforward. We are aware of the power of religious leaders too – of the Pope, the spiritual leaders of the Islamic world and in a similar but different way, religious leaders like the Dalai Lama. Then there is the power and influence exerted by rich and famous celebrities from film, the arts, and social media. This is all about leadership at an exalted level. We can look at the actions of these leaders, political, religious, and celebrity, and surmise that there is not a lot that you, me or our family, colleagues, and friends can do – to substantively affect what actually happens in the world given that our individual scope for influ-ehce is limited. Some will say that mass movements, pressure groups, global NGOs, and similar organisations of like-minded people – represent the way to go when it comes to changing things in the world we live in. And I would be the first to agree with that. And yet – there needs to be something else. I believe that that 'something else' is the way in which we lead and manage both ourselves and others in our own corner of the cosmos, influencing and affecting situations that are close to us and that we have an interest and a passion to change for the better. The American writer and organisational development specialist Margaret J. Wheatley has spoken eloquently of her attempts to work for systemic change, over a period of 20 years or more, but without feeling that she was managing to achieve much of what she had set out to achieve: it was relatively recently that she decided that her focus would shift more towards thinking about how individuals could develop what she referred to as deeper qualities, like compassion, in order to be able to change the way the world is. I like this quotation from Margaret for the sense of hope and possibility it conveys:

> *Relationships are all there is. Everything in the universe only exists because it is in relationship to everything else. Nothing exists in isolation. We have to stop pretending we are individuals who can go it alone. (Wheatley, 2002, p. 19)*

Margaret has also spoken in her many talks and lectures about the need to look beyond what she calls a Western mechanistic lens and to seek inspiration and ideas from untapped or relatively untapped sources.

One of these for me is the African philosophy of ubuntu which has gained recognition and popularity among leadership experts during the course of the past decade. Ubuntu has been elegantly explained by Archbishop Desmond Tutu:

> *One of the sayings in our country is Ubuntu – the essence of being human. Ubuntu speaks particularly about the fact that you can't exist as a human being in isolation. It speaks about our interconnectedness. You can't be human all by yourself, and when you have this quality – Ubuntu – you are known for your generosity. We think of ourselves far too frequently as just individuals, separated from one another, whereas you are connected and what you do affects the whole World. When you do well, it spreads out; it is for the whole of humanity.*

There is a commonality between what the Archbishop is saying here about ubuntu and what Margaret J. Wheatley has said. (Ubuntu was invoked in a speech by Barack Obama about Nelson Mandela too.) So I think this gives us a great starting point to think about how to develop as Expert Humans – this sense of interconnectedness – and it provides a rich seam of enquiry that encompasses not only altruism, compassion, and empathy (ACE) but also social network theory and the concept of weak tie networks – things we will come to during this course of this book.

If it is all about relationships, where do we start?

A good place to start, it seems to me, is to think about early life experience and what early childhood psychology has to say on the subject. One of my favourite psychologists is the Canadian professor of psychology, Dr Paul Bloom. He has pointed out how children from a very early age are able to show care and concern for others, explaining that one baby crying will very likely set off another baby crying as a show of support and empathy. Very small children will show worry and anxiety about another little child who is crying, by extending their hand and touching or by offering to share their toy with the troubled one. So it seems, as Professor Bloom (2018) points out, that we have the capacity and ability to feel and show compassion from a very early age. So when we meet people as adults who are lacking in compassion or who are in some way, dysfunctional in that area – what has happened to them? What life experiences have conspired to make them so different?

To start thinking about this, let's take a look at the work of John Bowlby.

John Bowlby (1907–1990) was a British child psychologist and the first of the Attachment Theorists. As such he was one of the key contributors to our understanding of early child development. His proposal was that the nature of the bonds children develop with a significant caregiver in very early childhood (or not) will have a profound impact on the rest of that person's life in terms of how they relate to other people. Bowlby's work and that of Mary Ainsworth in the 1970s and 1980s gradually led to the development of the concept of 'Secure Base', and eventually the extension of the concept to include adults.

This work has been further built on and developed by George Kohlreiser, Susan Goldsworthy, and Duncan Coombs (2012) in their book *Care to Dare: Unleashing Astonishing Potential Through Secure Base Leadership*. In the book, they define 'secure base' as:

> *A person, place, goal or object that provides a sense of protection, safety and caring and offers a source of inspiration and energy for daring, exploration, risk-taking and seeking challenge. (p. 8)*

One of the many reasons this is so important is that a secure base gives a person the inspiration and energy to be able to step out of their comfort zone and explore their unfulfilled potential, safe in the knowledge that their efforts to innovate and try new things, will be supported, and any failure they might happen to experience will not result in castigation or punishment.

A leadership style that is founded on secure base theory can also be helpful in navigating the disharmony and unpredictability of our times, whereby a leader with these qualities, strengthened by compassion and empathy, can provide a high degree of support and comfort to others, even though the leader herself will not be any clearer than anybody else in terms of what is going to happen next. While the atmosphere of uncertainty will undoubtedly persist, the calmness and 'solidity' of the leader is a welcome beacon of hope in choppy, uncertain waters.

ATTACHMENT THEORY AND ACE

In their paper, "Contributions of Attachment Theory and Research: A Framework for Future Research, Translation, and Policy" the scholars Jude Cassidy, Jason D. Jones, and Phillip R. Shaver (2013) suggest that while there has been a significant amount of research conducted by social/personality psychologists into adult attachment and prosocial behaviours:

> [...] the link between child attachment status and prosocial processes e.g. empathy, giving, and altruism has received surprisingly little research attention. (p. 19)

It seems clear that while some good work has been done in this area there is still more to know about how child development and significant caregivers (the presence or non-presence of) affects the future behaviour and interpersonal relationships of adults in the workplace. What is clear is that humans have an innate sense of ACE which is then developed – or not – as the child progresses into adulthood.

What is also so fascinating is this: given what we know already, what kind of life experiences shape and inform the development of ACE behaviours, and to what degree they are learnable? And in adulthood, how can underdevelopment of ACE behaviours be addressed?

We will explore this further in the next section.

WHAT 'HIDDEN GEMS' EXIST IN OUR HUMAN EXPERIENCE SUCH THAT WE CAN MAGNIFY AND DEPLOY THEM FOR OUR OWN GOOD AND THE WELLBEING AND RESILIENCE OF OTHERS?

'Don't have a mother', he said. Not only had he no mother, but he had not the slightest desire to have one. He thought them very over-rated persons. (J. M. Barrie, Peter Pan)

Peter Pan might be one of the most famous orphans in English literature along with Oliver Twist. But what about real famous people who were orphaned or put up for adoption?

Well these include Steve Jobs, Marilyn Monroe, John Lennon, and Leo Tolstoy. They all had unique talent and power and at the same time they were uniquely vulnerable too. Tolstoy was a father to no fewer than 13 children and yet it was said that he did not enjoy a good relationship with any of them. The lives of Jobs, Monroe, and Lennon are particularly well-chronicled so I will leave the reader to reflect on them. At the same time, I would suggest that they all wanted to make a mark on the world in some way. And they all appear to have had a series of relationships characterised by friction and disharmony. They were mavericks in a world that is both fascinated by and disapproving of people who are quite literally 'out of the ordinary'. We will return to this theme of 'out of the ordinary' in Chapter 5 when we look at neurodiversity and what Expert Humans can to do to help people who see the world differently to be protected, nurtured, and to thrive.

So what do we mean by 'hidden gems'?

I decided to use the term 'hidden gems' to denote those life events or experiences that shape us as altruistic, compassionate and empathic beings – or not. Hidden gems could be positive experiences that yield positive outcomes – or negative, challenging experiences that can be turned into positive ones as we grow and develop as adults and members of groups, teams, or organisations.

Among the negative and often traumatic experiences people can go through in early life is the loss of a parent. In her book, *The Fiery Chariot,* from the 1970s, the writer Lucille Iremonger noted the high incidence among British prime ministers of having lost a parent in their formative adolescent years. A total of 25 out of 40 prime ministers had suffered this loss, from Sir

Robert Walpole in the eighteenth century to Neville Chamberlain (the prime minister at the start of the Second World War). In the United States, we can discern a similar phenomenon: George Washington, Thomas Jefferson, Bill Clinton and Barack Obama all lost their fathers when they were youngsters. Abraham Lincoln lost his mother when he was only nine.

One contemporary British politician shared the following with the political journalist Isabel Hardman (2018):

> *My dad left my mother when I was very little and was barely involved, and so I have always had this endless desire to prove to him that I am actually worth knowing, that I've made something of myself. But because he's not around, I'll never satisfy that desire. So I just keep going. (p. 16)*

The author Malcolm Gladwell has also noted the same phenomenon, describing such individuals as 'Eminent Orphans'. Other notable examples of famous Americans who made it to the top despite early childhood tragedy are Supreme Court Justice Sonia Sotomayor and Bill de Blasio, Mayor of New York, who were 9 and 18 years old, respectively, when their fathers died.

Such sad events in the young lives of these famous and successful people should not lead to the idea that losing a parent early in your life is a guarantee of later (major) success. Rather they are examples of life events that shape people: these events give them a reason to push on (to prove they can 'make it') or affords them a kind of internal resilience that helps them manage future grief and setbacks. We might not want to call these tragic life events 'hidden gems' but to the extent they give some sense of worth and value to the individual as she progresses into adulthood, the fact of living through those experiences is something to admire and respect. There are also rather more positive 'hidden gems' which come from recollections of childhood – that are the polar opposite of what we have just looked at – and they too underscore the power and importance of 'secure base' in early life. In their study 'Retrospective Memories of Parental Care and Health from Mid to Late Life', William J. Chopik and Robert S. Edelstein (2019) noted the following:

> *People who have fond memories of childhood, specifically their relationships with their parents, tend to have much better health, less depression and fewer chronic illnesses as older adults. (p. 91)*

Chopik (2019) also points out that

> *memory plays a huge part in how we make sense of the world –*
> *how we organise our past experiences and how we judge how we*
> *should act in the future … we found that good memories seem to*
> *have a positive effect on health and wellbeing, possibly through the*
> *ways that they reduce stress or help us to maintain healthy choices*
> *in life.*

The researchers also noted that there was a stronger association for people when recalling their relationships with their mothers (insofar as mental health and wellbeing was concerned) in later life. Given the generational differences and the changing nature of parental caregiving in past decades, the researchers wondered whether fathers might start to feature more in this, as fathers in more recent years have had opportunities to spend more time with their young children than fathers in previous times. Another good reason for promoting paternal leave! And another good reason to recognise the power and importance of a secure base in early childhood.

When I was a child growing up in Uganda, East Africa – I had close to what people might call an idyllic childhood. Lots of racing around on bicycles with my friends, climbing up guava trees (and gorging on guava), exploring our town and the banana plantations nearby – it was a gentle, quiet period in my life. Then, one afternoon, my father called me in from the garden and announced that in two weeks' time I would be flying back to the United Kingdom on my own to go to a boarding school in South Wales. My mother would take me to the market that afternoon to buy towels and socks – and then affix the initials 'MJ' to all of them with an indelible ink marker. I didn't really have much time to process this decision and in those days a lot of decisions like this one were taken without very much consultation with the child in question (since the decisions were being taken with the best of intentions: 'It's for the best').

The sudden transition from the colours, warmth and vibrancy of East Africa to the browns, greys, and off-whites of an impending Welsh autumn in a fading seaside town on the South Wales coast – was quite a shock to the system. It took a while to get used to the new climate and new surroundings. I grew to quite like my school and my lessons, and in due course I made friends and started to settle in. The process of doing that, however, does require energy and self-reliance I think – since there is no one to turn to and in my case, my parents were far away in Africa. I think experiences like this stay with you forever and they shape who you are and who you become. I have always been self-sufficient, and I don't expect much from others. That said, when I ask for and I get help – then I am delighted! So what then about experiences in childhood and more specifically, experiences at work? What events shape us in those contexts?

One of the earliest books to tackle the subject of experience of work and the lessons we learn from being in the workplace was written by a group of researchers from the US-based Center for Creative Leadership and was first published in 1988. *The Lessons of Experience: how successful executives develop on the job* has become a classic, breaking new ground in terms of our understanding of how people learn at work and also, our appreciation of the significance of key events in the shaping of people's careers. *The Lessons of Experience* provided a jumping-off point for many further research initiatives as well as the creation of psychometric tools and coaching support materials. It enabled us to think about what kind of experiences people should actively seek out if they wished to strengthen a particular leadership muscle. The book's influence has been far-reaching: it has made a great contribution to the field of leadership development and coaching. I like to think that it has encouraged people to think about what 'hidden gems' (whether positive or negative) exist in their own life experience to date – and to use those hidden gems to help them develop and progress.

ATTACHMENT THEORY AND SAFE SPACES – HOW THESE IDEAS RELATE TO 'GOOD' WORK AND HOW WE CAN LEARN TO DEVELOP OURSELVES TO BE INSTRUMENTS FOR THE CREATION OF SUCH SPACES

We have already looked at the significance of attachment theory in early childhood development and the implications it has for a person's development into adulthood. We have considered the importance of 'secure base'. Building on this, we can start to think about the creation of 'safe spaces' in organisations – places where people can thrive, be happy, and feel fulfilled by what they do.

One of the main reasons people give for leaving a job is that the relationship with their immediate supervisor, their boss – was dysfunctional in some way. 'People leave bosses, not organisations' is a popular saying (to which not all people subscribe incidentally – some describe it as an 'urban myth' that it is the *principle* reason). I think people leave organisations for a variety of reasons – more pay, better development opportunities, a change of scene – these are just some of them. Having a lousy boss is not going to help a person to want to stay, though. So in terms of flight risk mitigation at the very least, it is critical to get that human aspect – 'good leadership' – to be as good as it can be. To me this means having managers and leaders who are able to create a safe space where 'good work' can occur: and by 'good work' I am referring to work which people find meaningful and satisfying. I think we can all recall hearing from friends who have worked for a boss who really didn't know what he was doing and who should not have been in that position. How on earth do they get there you might ask?

Well, bosses like these are sometimes people who have been promoted too soon and they are often people who really don't like or care for other people that much. Very frequently they lack self-confidence and more often than not, they lack self-awareness. These are two things which leadership development courses try very hard to develop, often with great success. In terms of bosses or leaders who don't really like people very much – I think these come in many different shapes and sizes and they vary greatly in how disagreeable they can be. Occasionally ordinary workers have the grave misfortune to cross the path of a corporate psychopath – woe betide you if you do. In studies of corporate psychopaths (hard-core narcissists who see others as pawns in an elaborate game of "people-chess"), we find that empathy is manipulated in such a way that our corporate psychopaths can 'read' others but don't have any feelings about them whatsoever. Sometimes corporate psychopaths show up as charming and they are often very funny – the life and soul of the party. They relish the game of 'gaslighting', slowly and carefully undermining the self-confidence of those they see as competitors, getting under the psychological skin of their colleagues. They chip away until their target begins to show self-doubt and gradually begins to lose confidence in their abilities. Eventually, the victim's sense of reality starts to weaken, enabling the corporate psychopath to deliver the final 'coup de grâce': 'we've lost confidence in you', which results in the unfortunate target of the corporate psychopath giving up and leaving.

A family friend working on a local newspaper, a woman in her mid-50s who loved her job, became the target of the newly appointed editor who, without losing much time, brought in his 20-something niece to be a cub reporter on the same team as the older woman. Little by little, bit by bit, the editor would question the choice of news story written by the older lady: why this story? It's not interesting. And then gradually, the editor began to question the older lady's command of written English: disputing word choices and asking for re-writes or for large chunks of articles to be deleted. It only took four months for the editor to get his way: the older woman began to suffer stress and panic attacks which required time off work – which was in turn used to justify to the owners of the paper that it was high time – in fact *appropriate* – to let the older woman go. Eventually, broken, she resigned and within days, the editor's young niece was promoted to Senior Reporter, Local News. The older lady never worked again.

This is why we must be on our guard against those who would use empathy for nefarious purposes and why we must bear in mind that empathy has a dark side too. Corporate psychopaths use themselves as an instrument to bully and torture others. We must call out such behaviour more assertively and emphasise again and again that this kind of thing is unacceptable in the modern workplace. Unfortunately, as I suggested in a 2016 article for *Global Focus* magazine published by the European Foundation for Management Development (EFMD), "The Global Workplace – A Compassion-free Zone?" – we truly have our work cut out. In the article, I mentioned getting feedback from a couple of men who had attended a conference at which I spoke about compassionate workplaces (or rather, the lack of them). They said that they had not been convinced by my arguments and interested, I asked them what they meant. They went on to say that it was not a question of liking or disliking my talk particularly, but that the nature of their workplace was such that it was about as far removed as one could imagine from being a caring environment as it was possible to be. They told me that the leadership in their company was cut-throat, highly political, narcissistic, and aggressive. You kept your head down and your thoughts and opinions to yourself – that is, if you wanted to get on. And so, given that their boss was a nightmare to work for, they were highly dubious that anything good could come of a situation like that and that anything to do with compassion wouldn't get off the starting blocks. I listened intently and have to say, I agreed with them. A culture characterised by fear and intimidation is shaped by the people at the top: it takes some time to create and it is not easy to dislodge or change once certain behaviours have taken hold. These behaviours are either tolerated or 'turned a blind eye to'. Amy Edmondson, in her book *The Fearless Organization*, does a great job of dissecting and analysing the various kinds of organisations where fear runs amok – including organisations where the rot is more insidious and takes longer to realise its destructive potential. Amy (2018) notes the following:

> *[…]a growing number of organizations are making the fearless organization an aspiration. Leaders of these organizations recognize that psychological safety is mission-critical…. (p. 103)*

During the course of *The Fearless Organization*, Amy points out that while there is an 'accepted narrative' (my words) around Nokia's troubles as the iPhone started to gain ground – that speaks to a slowness to react and an inability to innovate quickly enough – it was really the result of the toxic environment at that time, created by top leadership, which paralysed people and rendered them unable to challenge or confront the senior managers and directors about the direction of the company when in fact they ought to have been able to do so. Likewise the emissions scandal at Volkswagen was as much to do with fear as it was to do with lying: middle and senior managers were too frightened and felt too intimidated to say to their big bosses that what they were being asked to do was just plain impossible – let alone completely unethical (make diesel cars appear cleaner than clean in terms of their emissions). Given the choice between having your head chewed off in public and/ or getting fired, and falsifying emissions data – many people involved chose the latter. It was an example of group collusion and cohesion in service of a big corporate lie. If the leadership had not been so fearsome and so lacking in compassion or empathy, things might have turned out differently. It will take a long while for the Volkswagen brand and trust in the company to recover.

DEVELOPING OURSELVES TO BECOME INSTRUMENTS OF GOOD WORK AND SAFE SPACES

There is an aspect of OD (Organisational Development) called Use of Self (UoS) which is a wonderfully rich area to explore in connection with enabling good work and safe spaces. UoS looks at the self by taking a deep and intense approach – asking questions and challenging ourselves, inviting self-examination and self-reflection in a way that we don't often have the opportunity to enjoy or learn about, as much as we might like. The connections with ACE are also present too. Working on who we are and how we show up

Table 4: Johari Window.

	Known to Self	Not Known to Self
Known to Others	(Open Self)	(Blind Self)
Not Known to Others	(Hidden Self)	(Unknown Self)
Open	These are things (traits) that you and others perceive	
Blind	These are things that others see about you, but you do not	
Hidden	These are traits that you would include about yourself, but others would not	
Unknown	These would contain things that no one is aware of or knows about	

(at work, for example, but also in other contexts and situations) can help us to try to be the best versions of ourselves that we can be. The 'UoS' discussions sometimes reference the famous and insightful Johari Window model, created by the psychologists Joseph Luft and Harrington Ingham as a heuristic (diagnostic tool) to enable people to understand themselves better (Table 4).

There are Johari Window activities and exercises, often done as part of leadership development programmes, which help to shed light on how people see themselves and how others see them. This can be very useful in developing self-awareness and identifying potential areas for more developmental work. In Table 5, the adjectives contained therein are used to populate the grid as shown in Table 4. You might for instance describe your "Open Self" as "Friendly" (something others would perceive too). Your "Hidden Self" on the other hand might be described using the word "Tense" - something you would include about you, but others would not. And so on.

Table 5: List of Adjectives for Johari Window.

Able	Accepting	Adaptable	Bold	Brave	Calm	Caring
Cheerful	Clever	Complex	Confident	Dependable	Dignified	Energetic
Extroverted	Friendly	Giving	Happy	Helpful	Idealistic	Independent
Ingenious	Intelligent	Introverted	Kind	Knowledge-able	Logical	Loving
Mature	Modest	Nervous	Observant	Organized	Patient	Powerful
Proud	Quiet	Reflective	Relaxed	Religious	Responsive	Searching
Self-assertive	Self-conscious	Sensible	Sentimental	Shy	Silly	Smart
Spontane-ous	Sympa-thetic	Tense	Trustworthy	Warm	Wise	Witty

Working on our understanding of who we are and why we do the things we do is a great way to start thinking about how ACE might fit into the mix that creates each of us.

The thinkers and scholars Dr Mee-Yan Cheung-Judge and Prof. David Jamieson have done fantastic work in the area of UoS. Their thinking has greatly enhanced and advanced the understanding of the subject. Mee-Yan (2001) wrote in her paper, "The Self as Instrument – A Cornerstone for the Future of OD," about the need to 'own self':

> *In practice, owning the self means devoting time and energy to learning about who we are, and how issues of family history, gender, race and sexuality affect self-perception. It means also identifying and exploring the values by which we lead our lives, as well as developing our intellectual, emotional, physical and spiritual capacities. (p. 12)*

Fast-forward 17 years and we see the concept of UoS connected to *action* – which is something that is core to compassion and something which differentiates compassion from empathy (which does not necessarily imply action). To me, this is an exciting connection point: *to gain an appreciation of Self as a way to create mechanisms for specific types of actions and reactions in particular moments in time, and situations.* Mee-Yan, in a blog article in 2018 entitled "What more does OD need to do to become a 'must-have', 'desirable' function for Organisations?" also points out the following:

> *The concept of Use of Self is a core one for OD. As many writers (Nevis, Seashore, Jamieson, Cheung-Judge, Burke) put it – Use of Self is the way in which we act upon our observations, values, feelings and then intentionally execute an intervention necessary for the situation that presents. As we develop a heightened self-awareness, we allow our own sensations, feelings, knowledge and judgement to inform what action (or no action) we will need to take.*

What this tells us is that the pathway to developing ACE attributes requires at least two things: (a) knowing yourself, that is, *really* knowing yourself and (b) knowing what, if any, action to take, and when.

We will look at these ideas in more detail when we consider Altruism, Compassion, and Empathy in Chapters 6, 7 and 8, respectively. Just before we leave Chapter 4, these reflective questions from Dr David W. Jamieson are thought-provoking and great for reflection as we move on to further exploration:

- Our 'selves' are the primary instrument we use in the execution of our roles.

- They relate to all we do in our roles and what impact we have.

- We start with understanding self which is a social process involving others (feedback, what they can see and experience of us).

- It requires conscious presence to take in data from situations and ourselves, make sense of it, know our intention(s), see and create behavioural options and act with courage.

- Have reflective practices to learn from experiences in each action learning cycle.

- Each situation is the next opportunity to be your best self.

  – *Dr David W. Jamieson, Jamieson Consulting Group Inc., at the 2020 Annual Conference of ISODC (International Society for Organizational Development and Change Management)*

And just to underscore the importance of the role of self in enabling safe spaces and humane workplaces, here's what the protagonist in Haruki Murakami's 2002 literary masterpiece *Kafka on the Shore* had to say about safety, bearing in mind his bullying father:

I'm safe inside this container called me.

Our task is to help people feel safe inside *and* outside their container.

5

BREAKING NEW GROUND –
INTRODUCTION OF THE ACE MODEL

- Exploring 'weak tie' networks, their positive impact on human brain chemistry, and their contribution to our shared sense of humanity.

- Introduction of the new concept ACE – building the case for Altruism, Compassion and Empathy: business reasons for adopting ACE.

- Why we need the three (ACE attributes) working in combination.

- Moving across the spectrum – implications of neurodiversity on the workplace and the role Expert Humans can play in supporting people who see the world differently.

EXPLORING 'WEAK TIE' NETWORKS, THEIR POSITIVE IMPACT ON HUMAN BRAIN CHEMISTRY AND THEIR CONTRIBUTION TO OUR SHARED SENSE OF HUMANITY

Weak tie networks can be characterised as those relationships we have with a multiplicity of people whose names we are unlikely to know but who populate the landscape of our everyday lives. These are the baristas who greet you each morning with a cheery smile as they fix your order (from memory) or perhaps the bus driver who waves at you as you see your young children off to school. They could be the street cleaners outside your apartment or, if you live in a city like Singapore, they are the food court cooks and cleaners who recognise you for the regular customer you have become over time.

What happens in these small moments of kindness and friendliness is a reassurance that you are part of the world, taking up a bit of space and being 'seen' by others. This does positive things to your brain as it bathes it in feel-good chemicals. Such occurrences are very important for us: we know, for example, that elderly people often talk about not being noticed, as if no one would bother if they happened not to be around anymore. It is that feeling that you matter, even if it's only a feeling. People who are undergoing a depressive period can also start to feel that they don't really exist. So weak tie networks, for all their simplicity, are vital for our mental health. They also represent a subliminal reminder that we are part of something called humanity. I first noticed 'weak tie' networks a while back when reading a story from China about how promoting weak tie networks benefitted elderly dementia patients. Encouraging repetitive interactions with extended networks of the same people, establishing a daily pattern or routine and a effectively providing a reminder of what it is to be human – seemed to help slow the onset of the condition.

When I talked to a group of Human Resources directors about weak tie networks, I was struck by how they could see an immediate application of weak tie networks in their everyday work lives too: that for many of them, working in a large manufacturing plant let's say, or in an office block where there are usually hundreds of people from the same company working alongside each other – it's an extremely tall order to be able to remember everyone's name – until you realise that maybe you don't have to beat yourself up about it, and if nothing else, you can ensure that you make yourself visible, greeting people, asking them how they are and – smile. Trivial things one might say, but the science suggests otherwise. It will be interesting to see how the increased practice of WFH (Work From Home) will influence weak tie networks in the next decade.

In an article published online by Ian Leslie (2020), Ian points out the importance of a 1973 paper published by Mark Granovetter, a sociology professor at Johns Hopkins University called 'The Strength of Weak Ties' which, as Ian notes, 'Went on to become one of the most influential sociology papers of all time'. This was because:

> Until then, scholars had assumed that an individual's wellbeing
> depended mainly on the quality of relationships with close family
> and friends. Granovetter showed that quantity matters too ... one
> way to think about a person's social world is that you have an inner

circle of people whom you often talk to and feel close with, and an
outer circle of acquaintances whom you see infrequently or fleet-
ingly. Granovetter named these categories 'strong ties' and 'weak
ties'. His central insight was that for new information and ideas,
weak ties are more important to us than strong ones.

An example of this might be the way that a rumour travels. If you start a rumour among those friends with whom you have strong ties by sharing with just one friend, the chances are those friends will hear the rumour from each other and the rumour might just stay within that particular friendship circle. Likewise, most human beings are known to have a propensity to share a secret with *at least one other person* (even when the person who's being let in on the secret promises that the secret 'won't go any further'!) To get a rumour travelling really fast and wide, you yourself need to have a plethora of weak ties – or have friends who have them! In Granovetter's time (when he wrote his seminal paper), there was no Facebook, Twitter, Instagram, or LinkedIn. Today, these social media channels magnify the power of weak ties in a way that could never be achieved in pre-Internet days and as we know, they also have the power to project rumour and conjecture in a way never possible before. My interest in weak ties lies in the way that they can help individuals to feel connected, such that they help people with their mental wellbeing – and through this, increase the potential for positive knock-on effects in the workplace. The work of Granovetter and others takes weak ties into realms that also have other business implications for us. Some of these include how leaders are perceived by their followers; so to develop or gain trust in a leader that you have never met or might never meet (e.g., if you work for a huge multinational or a government) – is something that is more likely than not to come about via the power and influence of a myriad weak ties passing on impressions, recollections, gossip, and shared memories of interactions with the top leadership. Worth thinking about.

Weak tie networks can also be considered a subset of a bigger topic area: social networking. Social networking itself can be broken down into sub-categories too – such as the networking that occurs in a face-to-face way – and then of course social networking online. Granovetter is one scholar whose work has informed the creation of theories to explain social network-ing: another is professor Ronald S. Burt of the University of Chicago. Ron Burt delivered a lecture I was fortunate enough to attend when both of us were working at the business school INSEAD in Fontainebleau, France. Ron's

work is complementary to Granovetter's and fascinating in its exposition of
how social capital works in social networks. A key finding which fascinated
me is that in choices around performance evaluation and promotions, people
who have strong but 'closed' ties, that is, where their strength is limited –
tend to fare less well than those who enjoy a broader set of 'weak ties' which
are more open and extended. What Granovetter's and Burt's excellent work
doesn't cover (as it was not intended to) is to what extent social networks are
affected by altruism, compassion, and empathy. How might perceptions of
warmth and humanity about a particular person, as felt by people via a network of weak ties, be affected? Let me give an example. While I was working
at the business school INSEAD, one of my tasks was to help to put together
an event which we called The INSEAD Tokyo Alumni Forum (which took
place in 2008). The guest of honour and principal discussant was the then
rising star of Japanese business, the CEO of Nissan-Renault, Carlos Ghosn.
I recall how, as we awaited the arrival of this business superstar, all the staff
at the luxurious Hotel Okura were on tenterhooks wondering how the man
himself would 'show up'. What would he want to drink? Or eat? Where
best for him to sit? Mr Ghosn arrived at the agreed time and we set about
briefing him on what was going to happen next: going over once more (we
had informed 'his people' previously) what the timings would be and con-
firming (again) when the event would conclude. Someone then decided that
Mr Ghosn might be hungry and that sandwiches were to be ordered, and
fast. Within what seemed like seconds, a platter of sumptuous sandwiches
of all types and flavours appeared. But not just any old platter. This one was
the size of a small coffee table with maybe 50 sandwiches or more beauti-
fully arranged on it. Mr Ghosn by this time was seated on his own with our
INSEAD professor, with the rest of us standing around trying to look useful
and important. At that point, Mr Ghosn glanced up at us and said: 'Hey,
you guys must be hungry too, come, sit down, help me to eat these fantastic
sandwiches. Come!'

I like to think that this was a kind and generous invitation: it seemed so
out of kilter with the ferocious reputation Carlos Ghosn carried with him as
a ruthless cost-cutter who did not suffer fools gladly. (It has been interesting
to see how Mr Ghosn's life has developed since then). For me, he is the man
who shared his sandwiches with us and did a great job speaking at our event.
Experiences like these make you wonder how well anyone knows any of
these sorts of globally famous (or infamous) individuals, given how much we
are hostage to what we hear and read on the internet. And getting a sense of

their altruism, compassion, and empathy is not always easy either. I think it is the mark of an exceptional politician or country leader when they are able to reach through the void to touch people's hearts. Very few can do this in a sustainable and authentic way – as Expert Humans that is.

INTRODUCTION OF THE CONCEPT ACE – BUILDING THE CASE FOR ALTRUISM, COMPASSION, AND EMPATHY: BUSINESS REASONS FOR ADOPTING ACE

Let's have a look at something which I have named the ACE (Altruism, Compassion and Empathy) model (Fig. 2). These ACE attributes, as I call them, are *instances of humanity in action*. The evolution of this simple model began some eight years ago when I was thinking about what I thought made for an exemplary leader, given all the leaders I have been lucky enough to meet through my work, as well as all the leaders I have worked with (or 'for', as some of them would characterise the relationship). My work with ACE attributes started with a leadership model I began to develop – on a long plane journey from Singapore to London – which I called *Caring Charisma* – the 'Caring' part being about altruism, humility, and compassion; and 'Charisma' being an attempt to reframe and reposition Charisma as a positive attribute (given the negative reputation charisma has for many people – and especially people in the leadership development field). Superb writers and scholars like Tomas Chamorro-Premuzic have written eloquently and winningly about charisma in papers such as Tomas' own *The Dark Side of Charisma* (2016) in which he starts by saying:

Fig. 2: The ACE Model.

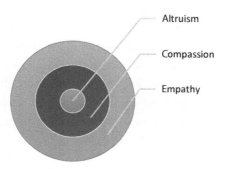

- Altruism
- Compassion
- Empathy

Most people think charisma is as vital to leadership as it is to rock stars or TV presenters and, unfortunately, they are right. In the era of multimedia politics, leadership is commonly downgraded to just another form of entertainment and charisma is indispensable for keeping the audience engaged. However, the short-term benefits of charisma are often neutralized by its long-term consequences. In fact there are big reasons for resisting charisma....

Tomas' perspective is balanced by others in the field who have worked hard and convincingly to have charisma be seen as a thing to develop and nurture. I have had the opportunity to attend a programme run by Nikki Owen based on her book *Charismatic to the Core – A Fresh Approach to Authentic Leadership* in which Nikki makes a strong case for taking charisma more seriously:

You don't have to shout or show off to be charismatic. Charisma is often seen as an intangible concept that unconsciously attracts a negative reaction in the world of business .... Life puts layers onto individuals, much like paint. When you strip away the layers ... when you are being true to who you are at your core – your charisma shines through.

My take on charisma was to try to understand what successful leaders got right that drew others to them. I thought it might be something like charisma. At any rate, I decided to corral my thinking into the model just mentioned – 'Caring Charisma' – which attempted to bring altruism, humility, compassion, and collegiality together with being engaging, strategic, focused, and pragmatic, and with all of these items being connected to ethics and morality, purpose, values, presence, and self-awareness. In 2013, I took this emergent model out on the road, that is, sharing it with business audiences, assessing their reactions, making changes and adjustments along the way.

It was through sharing and discussing this model with leadership development programme participants that I began to realise that of *all* the elements featuring in the model, the one that attracted the most attention was compassion. This was what made me eventually decide to set aside Caring Charisma for a while and to concentrate on studying compassion itself, in detail. From there I was very fortunate to be able to call on the support and assistance of Dr Meysam Poorkavoos of the Roffey Park Institute who became a comrade-in-arms for the further development of our shared understanding of compassion. We worked on the creation of a simple psychometric that people could complete on their phone in eight minutes or so – and then get an evaluation of their own compassion scores on five dimensions of compassion (comparing them to an existing UK norm group of around 500 people). This psychometric was popular with people attending our workshops on compassion, as it gave them a data point from which to start thinking about their own attitudes to compassion and how, if they were so inclined, they might consider changing their behaviour in some way or think about strengthening an existing core skill.

In the intervening few years since the work on compassion at Roffey Park, I have been back living and working in Asia. As my thinking on compassion has continued, so my interest in looking at how empathy fits into the picture – has developed too. And with the growing disruption we see in the world and the challenges we experience in dealing with disruption, it occurred to me that we might need to dial-up our concern for others – and that is what led me to start thinking more deeply about altruism. It was walking through a tropical rainforest with my wife that the thought of bringing the three things – Altruism, Compassion, and Empathy – together into a kind of 'Caring SuperTrio' – first came to me, and the notion of the three ACE attributes was born. I think people appreciate something tangible to hold onto when they are confronting the intangible: talking about ACE attributes makes such things more accessible and easier for people to start talking about (even though the thinking, feeling and emotion that sits under them can be extremely deep and highly complex). In other words, using the shorthand of 'ACE' enables us to fast-forward to having good conversations about interpersonal, human(e) relationships, and what we really mean when we interact – which is something I believe people are keen to explore deeply and – when they have found what they are looking for – are very often fascinated by and enjoy discussing. And who wouldn't? Talking about what makes us human has got to be one of the most fascinating topics of all time!

During my time presenting on compassion – and championing the cause of more human workplaces – I have found that for some people to get on board with the ideas, they really need to have some sort of 'proof of effect'. In their minds they want to know whether, if they invest some time in the subject of more human workplaces and engage in the notion of personal behaviour change – that it is going to be worth the effort. What's the ROI

(Return on Investment)? they ask. They want to be convinced of the concrete benefits that more ACE-oriented workplaces can enjoy. They also want to know that they themselves will be safe, as managers and leaders, if they try experimenting with new behaviours. I have often been asked: how can I be compassionate and yet hold my people accountable at the same time? Won't people think I am turning into a 'soft touch'? If I am going to make myself vulnerable in some way, how can I know whether it's going to be worth it?

So let's consider the ROI.

BUSINESS BENEFITS ARISING FROM ACE IMPLEMENTATION

In looking at business benefits, I think it is important to 'chunk them out' into the following categories of benefits (which are not exhaustive but intended as a starting point):

- Health benefits.

- Talent management benefits.

- Innovation benefits.

- Brand benefits.

- Customer benefits.

- Financial benefits.

In terms of *Health benefits*, I think we are all aware of the parlous state of mental health in workplaces around the world.

In their report on global mental health ('Mental Health') published in April 2018 (using data from 2017), Hannah Ritchie and Max Roser point out some of the challenges with arriving at reliable data – and emphasise that the data in their report are about prevalence rather than diagnosis, meaning that we need to exercise caution when making comparisons between countries or changes over time:

> For 2017 this study estimates that 792 million people live with a mental health disorder. This is slightly more than 1 in 10 people globally (10.7%). * (see also Fig. 3 for the situation in 2017).

Fig. 3:   Share of Population with Mental or Substance Disorders, Male versus Female, 1990–2017. The Chart Shows the Situation in 2017.

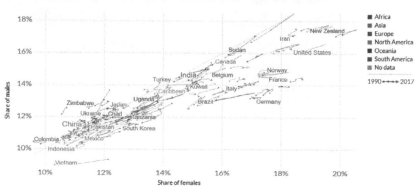

Mental health disorders are complex and can take many forms. The underlying sources of the data presented ... [require] specific definition ... in accordance with WHO's International Classification of Diseases (ICD-10) ... this broad definition incorporates many forms, including depression, anxiety, bipolar, eating disorder and schizophrenia. The data shown ... demonstrate that mental health disorders are common everywhere.

• Data in the report come from the Institute for Health Matters and Evaluation and are reported in their flagship Global Burden of Disease Study. The quotation comes from Our World in Data (which is supported by grants from the Bill and Melinda Gates Foundation and the Department of Health and Social Care in the United Kingdom).

*Data commonly used in the UK suggests that 1 in 4 people in England at any one time are suffering some form of mental ill-health (first reported via the annual mental health report 2016, shared by the BBC in January 2016).

For our purposes in *Expert Humans*, here's a chart which shows us the size and nature of the challenge (Fig. 4).

And just to provide a sense of what is covered under the term 'anxiety disorder':

Fig. 4:   Prevalence by Mental and Substance Use Disorder, World, 2017.

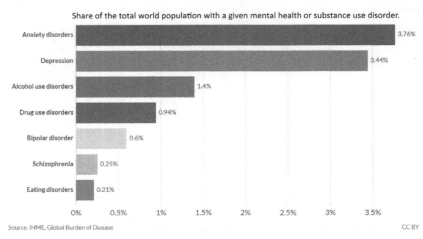

Share of the total world population with a given mental health or substance use disorder.

Source: IHME, Global Burden of Disease   CC BY

Anxiety disorders arise in a number of forms including phobic,
social, obsessive compulsive (OCD), post-traumatic disorder (PTSD)
or generalized anxiety disorders….frequent symptoms include
apprehension (feeling 'on edge', difficulty in concentrating); motor
tension (restless fidgeting, tension headaches, trembling, inability to
relax) and autonomic overactivity (light-headedness, sweating, dizzi-
ness and dry mouth).

• *Our World in Data*

From what we can see, there has to be scope to improve things. And while
there is no suggestion that ACE attributes are a panacea, the opportunity that
leaders have to shape workplaces that feel safe for people, where bullying
is eradicated and where there is no place for harsh or brutal managers –
through mindful use of altruism, compassion and empathy – has surely got
to be there. It has to be worth a try to put in place. It even has a business
imperative. According to *Forbes* magazine (2019), one in five Americans
suffer a mental illness each year and, 'Mental health and substance abuse
cost US businesses between $80 and $100 billion annually … depression
is thought to count for up to 400 million lost workdays annually'. In the
United Kingdom, mental ill-health costs the economy some £70 billion each
year and 91 million workdays are lost per annum.

Finding ways to reduce people's stress levels through better management and psychologically safer workplaces – has got to be the way to go. The Shaw Mind Foundation, a young charity working in mental health awareness and which specialises in mental health issues in the workplace and in schools, in both the United States and the United Kingdom, has this to say in terms of actions organisations can take to mitigate the potential for mental ill-health:

> *Some areas we suggest focusing on are:* • *Limiting working hours and out-of-hours email access.* • *Where possible avoid isolated work. If a person works from home then ensure regular check-ins with them.* • *Setting attainable deadlines and spreading the workload across teams.* • *Providing support services and staff members that are trained to deal with workplace stress.* • *Promote healthy eating and regular exercise.* • *The Shaw Mind Foundation* – Mental health and business: The cost of mental health and ways to reduce the impact on business (as reported by Carley Sime, writing in Forbes magazine)

It is note-worthy that the Foundation suggests we avoid 'isolated work' and that we 'ensure regular check-ins' with those working from home. This is an important point given what has happened as a result of the global pandemic.

In terms of *Talent Management benefits*, we know that attracting and retaining talented people is something that preoccupies everyone who runs a business, organisation or not-for-profit. Losing people is a huge cost derived from the cost of re-hiring; the cost of onboarding and training; the cost of learning and development and the cost of time with the role being left unfilled. This we know. The other thing we know is that throwing money at the problem won't solve it. Retaining people is about creating the right kind of environment, which is where the Expert Human approach with its emphasis on altruism, compassion and empathy can help.

In terms of *Innovation benefits*, a work atmosphere that is founded on psychological safety and led by managers who encourage and nurture – is likely to be one where innovation and creativity can flourish. John Ludema and Amber Johnson writing in *Forbes* magazine 'Avoid Risk, Make Innovation Possible: Psychological Safety As the Path To High-Performance' (24 September 2018) quote from an article by J. P. Davis and K. M. Eisenhardt (2011):

Not long ago, our attention was caught by an article on how tech companies innovate, patent new ideas, and take products to market.

It told the story of an engineer on a product innovation team that was struggling. The team faced a technical challenge, and the engineer knew of a simple solution using existing technology, but he decided not to share it with the others. He willingly withheld information.

Why? 'I didn't want to stick my neck out,' the engineer said.

He didn't feel safe sharing his ideas. The article doesn't elaborate, but maybe he felt he wouldn't get the credit for his hard work. Maybe he'd been criticised harshly in the past. Maybe he was worried the executive and experts on his team wouldn't believe that the junior employee could have the most elegant solution. Whatever his reasons, he didn't feel safe, so he kept quiet and the organisation lost out.

How many organisations must have missed out, like this one, because the atmosphere and the culture of the firm was such that fear was allowed to take hold?

And just to underscore the vital interplay between psychological safety – as a symbiotic element with trust and purpose – Natalie Turner, author of *Yes, You Can Innovate* and inventor of *The Six 'I's® of Innovation* observes:

Organisations that have a clear guiding purpose behind what they are trying to achieve, which is shared and agreed amongst team members, are more likely to create the psychological safety and trust that is fundamental for sustainable innovation to take place. We know that trust is foundational to feeling safe, and being willing to challenge each other's thinking, as well as feeling free to share new ideas, are of paramount importance if organisations are to encourage innovation from anyone, regardless of role or positional power.

An approach based on ACE attributes, therefore, creates a beneficial domino effect: ACE attributes support purpose, which in turn enables psychological safety and trust, which in turn leads to the development of a culture and atmosphere in which innovation can thrive. A virtuous circle is established.

In terms of *Brand benefits*, for companies and organisations which have been able to build a solid reputation for ethical behaviour, supporting equal opportunities and championing sustainable living, attracting people into the organisation is something that comes quite naturally to them. If organisations are able to project, prove, and live according to attributes such as altruism, compassion, and empathy, the potential for attracting and retaining top talent is certainly there. The appearance of apps such as Glassdoor, which enables employees past and present to evaluate their employer, makes brand reputation as a talent attractor even more powerful than it was in pre-app days. Social media has also meant companies having to keep on their toes, reputationally speaking, too. As we know, reports concerning the poor or exploitative treatment of employees don't take long to hit the headlines. Even in pre-internet days, careless talk and arrogant comments could cost you dear. In 1991 at an after-dinner speech in front of the great and the good of the UK business world, the jeweller Gerald Ratner joked about a couple of his company's products, deriding his company's sherry decanter as 'total cr-p' and explaining that its earrings were 'cheaper than an M&S (Marks and Spencer) prawn sandwich but probably wouldn't last as long'. The general buying public who had until then been happy if not proud to shop at Rattner's didn't see the funny side of things at all: they felt humiliated, made fun of. The now infamous gaffe cost Ratner 2,500 shops and his fortune as customers deserted him in droves. A 'Ratner moment' in the United Kingdom has now become synonymous with making a catastrophic gaffe. One can only imagine how distraught his employees must have been.

In more recent times, brands like Google have suffered when adverse news concerning staff gets top of the news billing, such as the 2017 reports about pay discrimination at the company. Facebook employees have attacked the company for its policies on fake news. All of these stories remain in the public consciousness long after they have peaked in terms of newsworthiness. I don't think many people have forgotten the words of the BP CEO Tony Hayward who at the time of the huge Gulf of Mexico oil spill said that he 'wanted his life back'. To his credit he issued an apology for the insensitivity of his remarks, but it is difficult to put the genie back into the bottle once it's out. And people remember.

As a one-time representative of my organisation at the CBI (Confederation of British Industry), I was always struck by how my business colleagues were keen that business be seen as a force for good in society rather than an exploiter of people. I definitely regard the vast majority of businesses as a force for good and I think that the more companies can embrace a more human approach to managing and leading people, the more people will react positively and show their loyalty by staying on, working hard, and recommending the company to their friends and colleagues. NPSs (net promoter scores) of companies by their employees are a carefully watched metric for some organisations, as they seek to keep their finger on the pulse of employee morale. This is one of many reasons for the rise in interest in 'the employee experience', arguably eclipsing 'employee engagement' as the management-speak phrase of the moment.

Customer and Financial benefits in some ways go hand in hand, with financial benefits accruing as a result of the organisation *being* more humane (based on ACE attributes). We can now show that organisations investing in their people by inviting them to take compassion training – achieve or exceed standard KPIs. This is something particularly noticeable in healthcare. In his paper on virtuousness in organisations in the United States, where virtuousness training includes what we would recognise as compassion training workshops, Professor Kim Cameron notes the following:

> *[A] study exploring causal associations between virtuousness and performance was carried out in 29 nursing units in a large healthcare system. A multi-year study was conducted to investigate the effects of organizational virtuousness on indicators of performance. Two findings of interest were produced:*
>
> *1. Units exposed to virtuousness training improved their virtuous practice scores significantly over the 2005 to 2007 period. Units not exposed to virtuousness training did not improve.*
>
> *2. Units improving the most in virtuousness also produced the most improvement in outcome measures. The two-year period saw double-digit improvements on most outcome measures included in the study. On each performance indicator, units that improved in overall virtuousness outperformed units that did not in subsequent years.*
>
> *From: Virtuousness and Performance: A Productive Partnership by Professor Kim Cameron, Stephen M. Ross School of Business, University of Michigan*

Kim Cameron, in his paper, also points out the concept of the 'eudaemonic assumption' which is that an inclination exists in all human beings toward *goodness for its intrinsic value.* This is where, for me, altruism comes in too. Virtuousness in Kim Cameron's definition is made up of three elements of which the eudaemonic assumption is one: the other two are the 'inherent value' (of virtuousness), namely that organisations and leaders should do good, because it is the right thing to do: and the third element is the positive, amplifying effect which virtuousness has as it permeates through the whole organisational structure. I have wrapped these ideas into an overarching idea of altruism, in other words, doing something for others without the promise of any expected benefit accruing to the person exhibiting altruism. What Kim Cameron is suggesting is that organisations that manage to integrate virtuousness practices into their work, will in fact benefit in a financial and performance improvement sense. Here is one more extract from Kim Cameron's (2012) report:

> *One study was conducted in the financial services industry. Stereo-typically, it is among the least likely industries to be interested in virtuousness because of its high-pressure, win-at-all-costs climate. Forty business units within a large northeast financial services company [in the United States] were investigated. The firm had embarked on a systematic effort to incorporate virtuous practices into its corporate culture in early 2005, when the CEO declared that a virtuous culture would guide the strategic direction of the firm. One year later, strong, statistically significant relationships were found between virtuous practices and six measures of financial per-formance. The following year, similarly significant associations were found between virtuousness scores, employee turnover, and organi-zational climate scores. Implementing virtuous practices produced the desired results.*

WHY WE NEED THE THREE (ACE ATTRIBUTES) WORKING IN COMBINATION

I believe that the creation of more humane workplaces is predicated on having the three ACE attributes working in combination, supporting and enabling each other. In the next three chapters of *Expert Humans*, we will be looking individually at altruism, compassion, and empathy: their histories, where they have come from, how they appear in practice and what we can do to promote and support them. The ACE model, introduced earlier, captures the following ideas:

- That Empathy is a wraparound attribute: feeling empathy is a natural precursor to compassion or the carrying out of a compassionate act – on its own however, empathy does not necessarily imply action. We can empathise with someone's (adverse) situation but it does not mean we are able to alleviate it.

- Compassion forms the main part of the ACE model – I like it because it has an action-orientation. Compassion is about alleviating the suffering of others and actively making things better.

- Altruism sits at the heart of the model and is an aspirational attribute. If we can do good then we should do so – as it is the right thing to do. Altruism is something we can harness to encourage a range of improvements to our disrupted world – with sustainability at the top of that list of improvements.

It is of course entirely possible for the three elements of ACE to happen independently of each other. My suggestion is that there is an inherent power in them when they all come together. I also think ACE attributes can be particularly helpful when it comes to supporting people with neurological difference, who see the world differently to the majority of us.

MOVING ACROSS THE SPECTRUM – IMPLICATIONS OF NEURODIVERSITY ON THE WORKPLACE AND THE ROLE EXPERT HUMANS CAN PLAY IN SUPPORTING PEOPLE WHO SEE THE WORLD DIFFERENTLY

Altruism, compassion, and empathy can be usefully deployed to help people with high-functioning autism and Asperger's to find their place in organisational life. Doing so allows society access to these unique talent sets. About 1% of the world's population have ASD (Autism Spectrum Disorder; details are available from the ASD Data, Center for Disease Control website); 80% of these people are unemployed and those that are in work are often given tasks that are menial and do not enable them to fulfil their potential. This is despite the fact that they often possess high intelligence and desirable qualities for employers, such as attention to detail and the ability to think outside of the box. We could all work a bit harder to bring people who see the world differently, into the world of work. And there are some great examples of this happening, enabled by altruism, compassion and empathy.

The leadership development consultant Sara Canaday writing in a post for *Psychology Today* (18 June 2017) has this to share:

> *I don't typically write or comment on issues of diversity and inclusion. But an often-overlooked aspect of the topic – cognitive diversity – is starting to come into the spotlight, and I have some insights on it because of the focus of my work. In my experience, I've seen that companies produce the best results and are better able to innovate when their team members don't all think, process information or see the world in the same way. Leaders who innovate and make an impact seek out those who don't share their opinions and resist the tendency to over-rely on their experience and what has worked in the past.*

I think there are exciting possibilities for us to apply ACE thinking in order to bring in people to our organisations who we might not previously have been minded to bring in (thinking that it would be too challenging, too difficult). To 'onboard' someone who has high-functioning autism requires a thoughtfulness, sensitivity, and preparedness that not all organisations are able to muster. If ACE attributes can become the bedrock of a corporate culture, we might look forward to the day when organisations become more tolerant of people who are different in the way they see the world are able to bring them in, and can ultimately achieve a win-win for all concerned. This is great for the organisation and great for the individual. Kristen Fellicetti writing for Monster.com has this to share:

> *Software corporation SAP has had its* Autism at Work *programme since May 2013, and HP and New Relic also have dedicated autism hiring programmes. Despite being a competitor to Microsoft, when SAP heard that Microsoft was setting up its own autism hiring program, they happily shared experience and insights. Kristen Fellicetti:* "These major tech companies are making autism hiring a priority"

What a first-class example of corporate altruism in action!

My hope is that we will be able to see more and more companies and organisations making the same journey.

6

ALTRUISM IN THE WORKPLACE

ALTRUISM – WHAT IS IT?

The word 'altruism' was first coined by the French philosopher Auguste Comte as *altruisme*, which he used to describe the opposite of egoism. He formulated *altruisme* from the Italian word *altrui*, which in turn came from Latin *alteri*, meaning 'other people', 'others', or 'someone else'. Put bluntly, altruism is the *moral practice of concern for the happiness of other people* and as such appears as a virtue in many cultures. It is also central to a number of world religions. Among the many interesting aspects of altruism, the notion of what constitutes 'others' can vary among different societies (and religions) and that is where one of the first challenges for society comes: how can we strengthen altruism so that we can be altruistic to people who are not like us? It seems that this is one of the fundamentals that we need to tackle. For this reason, it is necessary for us to think of ways in which we can deliberately set out to meet people who are not like us and hear their stories.

Easier said than done though. Many of us are quite happy to exist in our comfort zone of familiar faces and people – it makes for a less complicated life. We operate within a framework of 'weak tie networks' as described in Chapter 5 where we interact not just with people we know reasonably well – like co-workers or business acquaintances – but with an often vast array of people who are part of our personal landscapes – like the security guard or the food court cleaners or the barista in your local coffeeshop or server in a canteen – who we don't really 'know' at all. Our challenge is to throw the net wider and try to get to know and understand people who are beyond even our weak tie networks.

Altruism is an aspirational thing in many ways: taken to the limit and it becomes synonymous with selflessness, the exact of opposite of selfishness. We are a long way from reaching that stage, but at least we have something to aim for. And there's much to be gained by simply setting out on that journey. When you are gentle with an elderly person, for example, by asking them how they are today or by making a comment about the weather, or vacating your seat for them or seeing them safely across a busy street – you can be sure that what you are doing is way more than just *being kind*: you are helping a person feel that they matter and that they aren't invisible. This is very important especially (but not only) for elderly people and as mentioned earlier in *Expert Humans* – when people feel low or depressed it is often because they feel like they have ceased to take up space in the universe, that they are somehow redundant, unnoticed – and that it doesn't matter if they are around or not. For this reason, teaching ourselves (and starting with our children) that an act of generosity or kindness to others doesn't have to have any sort of payback – is a critical life lesson. It's a lesson that needs to be taught as vigorously and as often as possible.

ALTRUISM – THREADS IN PHILOSOPHY AND EVOLUTIONARY BIOLOGY

In addition to the contribution made by Comte to understanding altruism from a philosophical perspective, there is a fascinating history in the development of the concept of altruism from an evolutionary biology perspective – which we can trace back to Charles Darwin. It was something that exercised Darwin's mind as he put together his views on evolution during the writing of *The Descent of Man*. At one point, he fretted that the existence of altruism (which he had observed in animals) might represent a contradiction in respect of his major theory. How to accommodate the idea of the 'survival of the fittest' with the notion of sentient beings carrying out acts with no obvious benefit to themselves? A hundred years on and evolutionary biologists were still wrestling with the paradox as noted by Ian Johnston of The Independent in an article entitled 'Altruism has more of an evolutionary advantage than selfishness'. Johnston goes on to explain that in recent years, a team of mathematicians, led by Dr George Constable of Princeton University in the United States, have come up with a proof which they believe explains how and why putting yourself out for someone else can be better in the long run. They believe that altruism is 'real and developed' because it confers an evolutionary advantage that is ultimately greater than the benefits of selfishness.

The mathematicians used the example of 'Yeast'. Their logic runs as follows:

- Yeast produces an enzyme that breaks down complex sugars, creating more food for all.

- However, this requires expending energy that could otherwise be used for reproduction ....

- Which means that a mutant strain of 'cheaters' that selfishly avoids contributing to food production would *appear* to have a distinct advantage.

- However, too many cheaters and the food starts to run out!

- And the population crashes.

- A higher proportion of 'altruistic' yeast therefore means there will be *more* food and a higher population.

- So groups with higher numbers of 'altruists' are *better able to survive the random catastrophic events that happen from time to time.*

The neatness of this also means it can fit with Darwinian theory (if we wish to interpret it in a particular way). Altruism conducted on behalf of a group – to save the group – can be seen as contributing to the survival of the fittest *in its broadest sense.* What I loved about the yeast example was the idea that the higher the number of altruists, the better one's ability 'to survive the random catastrophic events that happen from time to time'.

And that time would seem to be now, given the disruptions in our world.

ALTRUISM – WHAT IT IS AND WHAT IT CAN SOMETIMES APPEAR TO BE

Table 6 is intended to map the different kinds of altruism we recognise, providing a definition and examples of what the term covers.

Table 6: Types of Altruism.

Type of Altruism	Definition	Examples
Altruism in general	Motivation to do good things for others	Can apply to the wellbeing of people, animals and the environment
Pure altruism	An act motivated purely out of concern for others	The desire to save an endangered species out of pure concern and empathy
Mixed altruism	Doing something partly motivated by altruism and partly by self-interest	Going to work in an animal shelter – partly to save animals but also to make a living
Weak altruism	A desire to do something good but not to the point of self-sacrifice	A wealthy person willing to donate cash but not their time
Inactive altruism	Altruism marked by inaction	A person who decides not to travel by air in order to help save the environment
Virtue signalling	Doing something for others out of a desire for recognition or publicity	Might be an example of mixed altruism. Celebrities adopting orphans might be an example
Humble altruism	Where you are unconcerned about promoting yourself	Anonymously giving someone an amount of cash to help them out
Self-sacrifice	Altruism that causes risk or loss to you	A bystander at a beach who dives in to save someone who is in difficulty
Selflessness	Being totally devoted to an altruistic cause and completely unconcerned with your own needs	Donating a kidney or vital organ to a complete stranger

Chart based on a post by John Spacey, 5 July 2020 for Simplicable.com and augmented by the author.

THE DARKER SIDE OF ALTRUISM

Pathological Altruism

Pathological altruism is a fascinating area of study which was brought to the fore by the editors Barbara Oakley, Ariel Knafo, Guruprasad Madhavan, and David Sloan Wilson in their book *Pathological Altruism*, published on 5 January 2012 by Oxford University Press. In a series of essays, the contributors explore the less positive side of altruism by explaining how, in certain cases, altruism incorrectly exercised can produce more harm than good. The authors underscore how carefully we should proceed when championing something like altruism – too much of a good thing can turn out to be highly detrimental, as we know:

> *Pathological altruism, in the form of an unhealthy focus on others to the detriment of one's own needs, may underpin some personality disorders. Pathologies of altruism and empathy not only underlie health issues, but also a disparate slew of humankind's most troubled features, including genocide, suicide bombing, self-righteous political partisanship, and ineffective philanthropic and social programs that ultimately worsen the situations they are meant to aid.*

Pathological altruism can also lead to co-dependency of a kind that results in some individuals defining themselves (who they 'are') in terms of the help and support they extend to, as well as the dependency they create, in others, manifesting itself in an obsession with caring for an ill person such that it becomes the focal point or fundamental meaning in the aid- or care-giver's sense of self-worth. In extreme and rare cases, explored in film and in fiction, pathological altruism gives way to Munchausen's syndrome by proxy (MSP) in which the person suffering from MSP seeks medical help for either made-up or exaggerated symptoms of a child under their care, while all the while intentionally making the symptoms worse through deliberate acts (such as poisoning, as depicted in the mini-series *Sharp Objects*). A condition such as this is extreme.

Paternalistic Altruism

Paternalism is typically when an authority figure decides what is best for you and believes him/herself to be acting altruistically, in your best interests. You don't get to decide anything, given that the paternalist makes all the decisions on your behalf – and does so in a more-or-less self-righteous manner. Authoritarian leaders often display this tendency and in the worst cases of abuse of power, they are quite capable of excusing themselves from the most horrendous crimes (on the basis that they felt themselves to be acting altruistically and of course, in the best interests of the nation). The deadliest combination I think we have seen historically is when narcissism meets paternalism (or paternalistic altruism). Unfortunately for the countries they rule, we also have a number of such people in charge of them today.

Table 7: Altruism in Global Religions.

Religion	How Altruism Features	What We Can Learn
Buddhism	Features strongly in all Buddhist traditions, especially Tibetan Buddhism, along with compassion and love	The Dalai Lama: 'The more we care for the happiness of others, the greater our own sense of wellbeing'
Christianity	A recurrent theme in the Bible is that people should give of themselves without any expectation of personal gain	The story of the Good Samaritan is a great example of altruism in action
Hinduism	Selflessness, devotion and duty are emphasised	Nonviolence is the key precept in Hinduism
Islam	Holds altruism in high esteem – known as 'esaar' or 'ithaar'	The maxim is to prioritise others over yourself
Jainism	Built around altruism in many respects	Preaches the view of 'Ahimsa' – to live and let live, not harming other living beings/entities
Judaism	A guiding principle in Jewish ethics is to love your neighbour as you would yourself	The purpose of human life is service in the here and now. Set aside ego and work for others
Sikhism	Altruism is a central tenet of the religion	'Seva' or selfless service to the community is key

ALTRUISM AND OUR WORLD RELIGIONS

I have mentioned how altruism features in our world religions. In Table 7, we share what is common between those global religious traditions.

ALTRUISM IN INTERCULTURAL CONTEXTS

One interesting study, "Cross-cultural Assessment of Altruism and its correlates," by Ronald C. Johnson and colleagues, published in 1988, looked at altruism in university students in six different locations: the United States (Hawai'i), the United States (Missouri), Egypt, Taiwan, South Korea, and what was the old Yugoslavia. The study hypothesised that group income or access to resources would be positively associated with giving and receiving help – but this was not the case: countries with relatively low access to resources like Egypt but which have high altruism scores, show that being rich or being poor is not a bar to being altruistic or displaying altruistic behaviours. As we know from the chart above, Islam treasures altruism, given that one of the five pillars of the religion is charity (with charity towards people to whom you have no obligations, being particularly highly regarded). In contrast, Taiwan and South Korea are examples of cultures with a substrate culture formed by Confucianism. These cultures are more typically concerned with obligations and the emphasis is on assisting family members or people within a close 'in-group', rather than helping those who we might identify as 'non-kin' or 'out-group'.

Another interesting finding in this research was this:

> *Sex differences are present both for the altruism scale as a whole and for different types of giving help, with almost all of the differences showing males to be more altruistic ... almost without exception our items were phrased in terms of helping strangers or acquaintances ... [and] it is with regard to this kind of helping that males have been found to be more helpful, while females are more helpful than males to persons with whom they have close relationships.*

The study doesn't speculate on why this might be so: it is a study of university students with a certain shared experience and as such it would be good to look at a broader demographic and to add more countries into the mix to test how consistent the findings from 1988 might be.

ALTRUISM IN SOCIETY AT LARGE

In a 2003 report by Tom W. Smith of the National Opinion Research Center/ University of Chicago Report prepared for the Fetzer Institute entitled: "Altruism in Contemporary America: A Report from the National Altruism Study," the author noted that at the time:

> *One of the main limitations of social science research on altruism is that most research has been based on very restricted, small, non-representative samples, mostly of undergraduate students ... To expand knowledge about the level, nature, and associates of empathy and altruism in American society, measures of these constructs were placed on a national, full probability sample of adult Americans.*

The results make for interesting reading (within the context of it being a snapshot about American altruism some 17 years ago): the researchers found that empathy and altruism in terms of *values* – were more widely held by women than by men: however when considering empathy and altruism as *behaviours* – there was no difference in gender. This is important because it adds strength to the argument that from a behavioural perspective, there is no difference in what we should be able to *expect* from men or women. In terms of what differences might exist, here's an interesting perspective from a 1990 research paper by Jane Allyn Piliavin and Hong-Wen Charng of the Department of Sociology at the University of Wisconsin entitled "Altruism: A Review of Recent Theory and Research":

> *Eagly and Crowley (1986) argue that sex differences in helping behavior are derived from social roles occupied by men and women. Women report providing their friends with more personal favors, emotional supports, and counselling about personal problems than men do (Aries & Johnson, 1983; Berg, 1984; Johnson & Aries, 1983). Helping expectations for men are associated with nonroutine and risky actions and protective roles. Using meta-analysis, they found support for social role theory in explaining differences in males and females. Their predictions were confirmed that 'men should be more helpful than women to the extent that (a) women perceived helping as more dangerous than men did, (b) an audience witnessed the helping act, and (c) other potential helpers were available'. Sex differences in helping behavior may be due to gender-related traits of masculinity and femininity, rather than to sex per se or to gender roles.*

ALTRUISM IN BUSINESS

In 2019, Larry Fink, the Chairman and CEO of the American multinational investment management corporation BlackRock memorably issued his famous letter to the CEOs which looked at purpose and its compatibility with profit. It was a call to action to put purpose at the centre of business. In his 2020 letter to CEOs, he addressed a number of other critical issues including sustainability. BlackRock wields enormous power and influence and in his letter, as reported by the journalist Wes Schlagenhauf, Mr Fink pulled no punches:

We believe that when a company is not effectively addressing a mate-
rial issue, its directors should be held accountable. Last year Black-
Rock voted against or withheld votes from 4,800 directors at 2,700
different companies. When we feel companies and boards are not pro-
ducing effective sustainability disclosures or implementing frameworks
for managing these issues, we will hold board members accountable.
Given the groundwork we have already laid engaging on disclosure,
and the growing investment risks surrounding sustainability, we will
be increasingly disposed to vote against management and board direc-
tors when companies are not making sufficient progress on sustaina-
bility-related disclosures and the business plans underlying them.

Mr Fink is nothing if not a realist in what he says. My reading of his
words suggest that companies not only need a call to action, but they also
need to be aware of the consequences of not taking action. Altruism seems to
be a last resort – certainly for these companies! To be fair, however, it's not
the same across the board so to speak – as there are a number of organisations that have become standard bearers for a different way of doing business that looks more like the altruistic approach that I have in mind. In an
article in *The Guardian* on 6 June 2014 entitled: "Can altruism be good
for business?" Professor Lynda Gratton of London Business School outlines
the case of The John Lewis Partnership in the United Kingdom and Danone
in Bangladesh where both companies provide great examples of 'corporate
altruism' that is also good for business. In the case of The John Lewis Partnership, the company is keen to support local community initiatives in a
manner envisaged by its founder. In the case of Danone, the CEO of the company collaborated with the head of famous micro-financing Grameen Bank,
Muhammed Yunus, to look at ways to encourage economically sustainable
businesses in Bangladesh. As Professor Gratton explains:

The company's first yoghurt plant in Bogra, Bangladesh now
employs 117 full-time employees, drawn from local communities
in a region of extreme unemployment. It also employs over 800
Danone sales representatives who take yoghurt to be sold individu-
ally to people in the neighbouring towns and uses milk from over
370 micro farmers from around the region. Without a dairy plant,
the milk these farmers produce typically goes no further than the
village and is the victim of unpredictable demand. The plant helps

ensure that their milk is sold every day, and the fixed price encour-
ages them to make future investments in their cattle. This social
business model has been extended to other regions across the world,
including Senegal and Algeria.

    Lynda Gratton, 6 June 2014, 'Can altruism be good for business?'
published in The Guardian.

These are good examples of companies acting in a way that is both altruistic and makes sense from a business point of view. But just how prevalent
is altruism really, among corporates?

In a World Economic Forum report by Isaac Getz, a professor at ESCP
Europe Business School and Laurent Marbacher, an author and consultant,
entitled *Altruism can be good for business, as these companies show*, the
writers examine two companies to try to get under the skin of what makes
for an altruistic commercial enterprise. One is the Swedish bank Handelsbanken and the other is the Japanese pharmaceutical multinational, Eisai.
The authors write:

[...] [There are some] practices [which] may seem bizarre
– indeed, altruistic – for capitalistic businesses, but there's
more. First, these, and other companies we have studied, don't
limit their altruism to one of a few actions of that kind per year.
They do it all the time. In fact, they strive to transform all their
business activities to create social value. Second, by uncondition-
ally pursuing social values as best as they can possibly do it, they
outperform their traditional competitors who are only focused on
financial results.

The authors also flag the existence of the *obliquity principle* proposed by
John Kay, a British economist, in 2004, which states:

If you want to go in one direction, the best route may involve going in
the other. Paradoxical as it sounds, goals are more likely to be achieved
when pursued indirectly. So the most profitable companies are not the
most profit-oriented, and the happiest people are not those who make
happiness their main aim. The name of this idea? Obliquity.

So, altruistic corporations do just this: they focus exclusively on social
value creation and by doing this, they turn out to be successful from an economic or financial perspective too.

HANDELSBANKEN

Handelsbanken is the oldest member of the Swedish Stock Exchange. Here's what the bank has to say about its position on sustainability and its attitude to customers and business:

Our commitment

> At Handelsbanken, we understand the impact we have on society, the environment and the financial market. Taking responsibility and looking to the long term have been core values guiding our work over many decades.

> Strong and lasting business relationships, low risk-taking and cost-awareness are cornerstones of our business. We have integrated this sustainable thinking for so long, it has become natural for us. Our financial strength helps us to avoid becoming a burden on society when times get tough. Instead, we can positively contribute by being financially stable. We always want to be close to the community where we operate, close to the customer.

> We have significant responsibilities, and we are committed to living up to them.

Perhaps this is one of the closest examples we can find when it comes to what I might call 'true corporate altruism' rather than the 'mixed altruism' of many organisations (which do good CSR (Corporate Social Responsibility) deeds and gain commercially at the same time). The wellspring for Handelsbanken's altruism comes from a combination of purpose ('taking responsibility') and a certain degree of 'sticking to the knitting' ('Our financial strength helps us to avoid becoming a burden on society when times get tough').

EISAI

The Japanese healthcare group Eisai is an excellent example of a company aspiring to great things. It is also what I would consider a fine exemplar of altruism in a corporate setting.

Here is the exposition of the company's *hhc* ('*h*uman *h*ealth *c*are') philosophy (Fig. 5). Note the sentence:

Fig. 5:   Eisai's hhc Logo.

'[...]it is important for each employee to first get close to patients and see the situation through their eyes to learn to pick up on thoughts and feelings that might not necessarily always be expressed in words' [a clear reference to empathy]:

Eisai's corporate philosophy includes the realisation of human health care (hhc). *Based on a clear understanding that patients as well as their families and consumers are the key players in health-care, we seek to have a sense of pride in providing benefits to such persons. This philosophy is summarised by the term 'hhc'.*

We believe that in order to truly consider the perspectives of patients and their families, it is important for each employee to first get close to patients and see the situation through their eyes to learn to pick up on thoughts and feelings that might not necessarily always be expressed in words. It is this concept that is the starting point for all of Eisai's corporate activities. Accordingly, the Eisai Group recommends that all of its employees spend 1% of their working hours with patients.

Our corporate philosophy is understood and internalised by each employee within the Group, both in Japan and overseas. This understanding is then shared and implemented in the daily business activities of all Eisai employees, and serves to effectively transcend nationalities, national borders, and gender and age.

We fulfil our obligation to society by considering the perspectives of patients, their families and the global community overall, developing a response to their needs, verifying the social benefits of this response, and finally by making this response available to the world before anyone else. This is the hhc that Eisai aims to realize.

I think Eisai sets the bar high. It's a role model for companies who are becoming more aware of their place in society and how they might want to change it for the better. It's also worth noting that the logomark of Eisai's *hhc* is written using the handwriting style of Florence Nightingale (1820–1910), who – as Eisai mentions,

> *'Made enormous contributions to the development of the nursing pro-fession and public health ... [a] prominent figure, who we regard as having played an immense role in the history of modern-day nursing'.*

ALTRUISM AND YOU

So how altruistic are you? A way to ponder this question is to look at completing a self-reported assessment. One of the earliest examples of such an instrument is reproduced below. This was devised by J. R. Rushton, R. D. Chrisjohn, and G. C. Fekken in 1981 and forms part of their study "The altruistic personality and the self-report altruism scale" in *Personality and Individual Differences,* 2, 293–302. Subsequent studies of altruism have built on this early assessment tool and tailored it to suit different cultural contexts and situations (such as replacing the item: 'I have helped push a stranger's car out of the snow' with 'I have helped get a stranger's car started', etc.). As with all assessments, getting the results is only one part of the exercise – figuring out what to do about them and taking appropriate action – is even more exciting and useful. Such self-reported assessments can form the basis of rich coaching discussions too – around why one might have answered a particular question in a particular way, and what the implications of that might be.

Table 8 provides an example of what a self-report altruism scale looks like.

The Self-Report Altruism Scale

Instructions: Check the category on the right that conforms to the frequency with which you have carried out the following acts.

Table 8:   Self-Report Altruism Scale.

	Never	Once	More than Once	Often	Very Often
1. I have helped push a stranger's car out of the snow					
2. I have given directions to a stranger					
3. I have made change for a stranger					
4. I have given money to a charity					
5. I have given money to a stranger who needed it (or asked me for it)					
6. I have donated goods or clothes to a charity					
7. I have done volunteer work for a charity					
8. I have donated blood					
9. I have helped carry a stranger's belongings (books, parcels, etc.)					
10. I have delayed an elevator and held the door open for a stranger					
11. I have allowed someone to go ahead of me in a lineup (at photocopy machine, in the supermarket)					
12. I have given a stranger a lift in my car					
13. I have pointed out a clerk's error (in a bank, at the supermarket) in undercharging me for an item					
14. I have let a neighbour whom I didn't know too well borrow an item of some value to me (e.g., a dish, tools, etc.)					
15. I have bought 'charity' Christmas cards deliberately because I knew it was a good cause					
16. I have helped a classmate who I did not know that well with a homework assignment when my knowledge was greater than his or hers					
17. I have before being asked, voluntarily looked after a neighbour's pets or children without being paid for it					
18. I have offered to help a handicapped or elderly stranger across a street					
19. I have offered my seat on a bus or train to a stranger who was standing					
20. I have helped an acquaintance to move households					

Source: Rushton et alv. (1981).

WHERE NEXT FOR ALTRUISM?

It is clear from our examination of altruism in this chapter that our understanding of the topic is evolving, given that different people will approach it from different professional angles. As Jane Allyn Piliavin and Hong-Wen Charng of the Department of Sociology at the University of Wisconsin said back in 1990, in Altruism: "A Review of Recent Theory and Research:"

> [...]for a long time it was intellectually unacceptable to raise the question of whether 'true' altruism could exist. Whether one spoke to a biologist, a psychologist, a sociologist, an economist, or a political scientist, the answer was the same: Anything that appears to be motivated by a concern for someone's needs will, under closer scrutiny, prove to have ulterior selfish motives.
>
> In all of these areas we are now seeing 'a paradigm shift'.

This paradigm shift started 20 years ago. I believe we are coming to a point where people and organisations are realising that altruism is something that we can invite ourselves and others to consider more in our daily lives – and in the workplace.

Given that we are experiencing a period in human history which will continue to be marked by significant disruption, we will be increasingly called upon to tackle challenges and situations that require a more altruistic approach. In this chapter, we have looked at different types of altruism and the place of altruism in world religions; we have looked at organisations which get as close to an altruistic positioning as one might hope for: a kind of 'mixed altruism'. What I have found is that – despite some fantastic examples – there is still a global dearth of organisations that are truly embracing the concept of altruism in the sense that it is now generally accepted, which is to do good without promise of payback to the altruist.

Piliavin and Charng had this to say in 1990:

> Our conclusion from the limited literature we have been able to discover on corporate responsibility is that 'enlightened self-interest' rather than altruism is what drives socially responsible behaviour in this area. Normative pressures can increase social responsibility, largely because such pressures lead corporate officers to perceive that socially responsible behaviour is in the corporation's own best

interest. Although individual corporate officers may feel empathy or have 'group-oriented feelings', corporations obviously do not. The behavior of these corporate officers, acting for the corporation, must be largely determined by the self-interest of the company. If altruism is seen as based on their feelings, then corporate philanthropy is not and cannot be altruism.

I think we can accept that corporate philanthropy is not the same thing as altruism. But we still need to encourage *corporate altruism*, which can only be created and shaped by the leaders of the organisation.

The biggest disruptor we face is the sustainability of the planet. If ever there was a time to appeal to the sense of altruism of our business and political leaders, it is now. And to give altruism more of a chance of success, I believe we would do best to combine it with compassion and empathy.

This will require the development of new leadership skills for our disrupted world.

7

COMPASSION IN THE WORKPLACE

COMPASSION – AN OVERVIEW

When I started researching and investigating compassion the best part of eight years ago, some colleagues at work (in a leadership development organisation in England) were sceptical about the subject. One even said: 'Michael, none of our clients are interested in compassion. None of them are asking for it'. I decided to persist with my interest in the subject and simply weathered the ongoing criticism that we should not be concerning ourselves or wasting time on something as pink and fluffy – and frankly as useless to organisations – as compassion.

Thanks to other like-minded friends and colleagues, however, we began to make some progress in terms of our understanding of compassion, discovering along the way – and to our delight – that there were others around the world who were also taking a serious look at the role of compassion, particularly compassion at work. Today, compassion is really coming to the fore.

PRE-REQUISITES FOR COMPASSION TO EXIST

One contribution I would like to share comes from the *Oxford Handbook of Positive Psychology* edited by Eric Cassell (2009) which offers up a thought-provoking set of three major requirements for compassion to exist. Here they are:

People must[...]

- *Feel that the troubles evoking their feelings are serious*

- *Understand that sufferers' troubles are not self-inflicted*

- *Be able to picture themselves with the same problems, in a non-blaming and non-shaming manner. (pp. 393–403)*

From this, we can see that compassion is all about *active alleviation of the pain experienced by another person*. It's about meeting people where they are and avoiding a tendency (which we often have) to be instantly judgmental. When your friend shares with you the pickle they are in – as a result of a number of stupid decisions he or she has made – it is often quite hard not to think: 'Well, this is all your own fault. You've made your bed, now you need to lie in it'. It requires us to suspend judgement and to think about *how* to help. This active quality is what marks compassion out when compared with empathy (which we will look at in Chapter 8).

DECONSTRUCTING COMPASSION

During the past few years, I have spent time thinking about how to deconstruct compassion into more accessible pieces – building on work that my colleague Dr Meysam Poorkavoos and I did at Roffey Park Institute some five years ago. At that time, it had become apparent that business audiences and participants on leadership programmes wanted a way to understand compassion such that they could address those parts of their leadership skills repertoire that might be lacking in one or more of the compassionate leadership sub-components. Being aware of these components and how they show up in a given person – was a good way to zero in on and focus on things that as leaders, people might want to change about their approach to leadership and specifically, to adopt a more compassionate leadership skillset.

The research literature variously subdivides compassion into five or six components or elements. In our work at Roffey Park Institute, we opted to concentrate on five areas, namely (1) Being alive to the suffering of others, (2) Being non-judgemental, (3) Being distress-tolerant, (4) Being empathic, and (5) Taking appropriate action. The key thing to share at this point was that we made a clear distinction between compassion and empathy, regarding the latter as a pathway to the former. In other words, while empathy is a hugely important attribute, it doesn't have the same action qualities as compassion. It also has a dark side too, which we will explore in Chapter 8. We also considered the importance and impact of self-compassion – of which more later in this chapter.

A paper by Clara Strauss et al. (2016) builds on the researcher Paul Gilbert's concepts of distress tolerance and non-judgement:

> Distress tolerance *is defined as the ability to tolerate difficult emotions in oneself when confronted with someone else's suffering without becoming overwhelmed by them. Gilbert argues that this is important because if we over-identify with a person's suffering we may feel a need to get away from them or reduce our awareness of their distress, preventing a compassionate response. This suggests that, although compassion is about 'suffering with' another person, if we feel such extreme personal distress in the face of another's suffering that we become too focused on our own discomfort, this may hinder our ability to help.*
>
> *The final element of Gilbert's model –* 'non-judgement'– *is defined as the ability to remain accepting of and tolerant towards another person even when their condition, or response to it, gives rise to difficult feelings in oneself, such as frustration, anger, fear or disgust. The idea that compassion means approaching those who are suffering with non-judgement and tolerance–even if they are in some sense disagreeable to us – is also central to Buddhist conceptualisations. For example, the Dalai Lama (in 2002) contends that:* 'For a practitioner of love and compassion, an enemy is one of the most important teachers. Without an enemy you cannot practice tolerance, and without tolerance you cannot build a sound basis of compassion'. (p. 17)

So compassion is all about doing something to (1) alleviate someone's distress or suffering, (2) make life better for another human being or group of people, and (3) understand where others are in order to help them to improve their circumstances or situation. This is why compassion can play a critical role in developing people in many different and positive ways: it is where coaching and mentoring (people to be more compassionate and caring) –

can be of huge benefit and impact. Paul Gilbert (referenced above) has also pointed out that 'Compassion breeds compassion' (in *Compassion Focused Therapy*, Routledge, 2010).

MORE ON COMPASSION IN THE WORKPLACE

My work on compassion with Dr Meysam Poorkavoos at Roffey Park Institute was included in a 2017 UK national initiative around the promotion of more compassionate workplaces by the National Forum for Health and Wellbeing at Work called *The Compassion at Work Toolkit*.

I wrote in the conclusion to the Toolkit:

> *There is still a mountain of indifference or scepticism about the positive effects of compassion at work that together, we need to tackle. For too long we have ignored the toxic effects of poor or aggressive management in the UK: for many organisations, so-called high performers have been allowed to continue with their bullying ways, immune to action by managers fearful that they will be unable to reach the stretch goals, KPIs or levels of profit demanded by stakeholders, without such individuals. This needs to change. We need to challenge the status quo and make it clear that enough is enough and that a radically new way of looking at things, indeed a radical new way of being, is what is required.*

I think there are definitely signs that people are taking compassion in the workplace more seriously: for example, discussion about mental ill-health at work happens more often these days, which is a good thing (not often enough probably, but this is an improvement nonetheless). I do not, however, think that we have really shifted the needle much in the past three years since I wrote those words: at best awareness of the importance of compassion and empathy is on the rise – but there is a lot more to do. What has been underscored for me since moving back to Asia is that the lack of compassion in the workplace is far from being a phenomenon that only impacts a country like the United Kingdom. It is everywhere.

Fig. 6 illustrates what some of the issues confronting the development of compassion in the workplace are (*Compassion at Work Toolkit, National Forum for Health and Wellbeing*, 2017).

Fig. 6: Issues Confronting the Development of Compassion in the Workplace.

Anyone with the experience of the workplace will have come across one or more of the items above playing out in the organisation. My suggestion is that fostering more compassionate leadership among our leaders – could be one worthwhile way to address some of the issues we encounter.

COMPASSIONATE LEADERSHIP

In the world of work, it is encouraging to see more leaders practising what has come to be termed 'compassionate leadership'. The *Financial Times* recently noted the following:

> *[Regarding compassionate leaders] ... in a recent survey of people affected by the [COVID-19] pandemic, 90% of participants felt such leaders improved their work-life balance and job satisfaction. And 70% of those who worked for compassionate leaders were more productive than those who didn't.*
>
> Financial Times *12 May 2020.*

Progress of a kind. At the same time, I think we are far from see-ing compassion as a hard-wired corporate attribute. In early 2020, the ride-hailing app Uber fired nearly 3,700 employees, representing 14% of its workforce, via multiple Zoom calls; each call took less than 180 seconds and had a brutally succinct message: 'Today will be your last working day with Uber'. Reports described how when the call started at 10:30am employees were greeted with a 5-minute silence and a static slide saying 'COVID-19'. Some thought they were experiencing technical difficulties and decided to leave the call. They were unable to get back in. Had they waited and not left, they would have been witness to what has to be one of the coldest, compassion-free company announcements ever: 'Today will be your last working day with Uber'*. Not much compassion in evidence there.

*Anushree Sharma, People Matters: *Uber fires 3,700 employees over a zoom call 14 May 2020.*

Scholars around the world have carried out studies that show that more compassionate workplaces bring a wealth of benefits to employees and customers alike. Commitment to the organisation and strong engagement are just some of the hallmarks of a compassionate organisation. Mental health improves as employees feel more able to discuss their issues with both their bosses and their co-workers. Importantly too, psychological safety increases – and with it, firms become more innovative and creative as employees feel free of the risk of castigation if they get something wrong. Everyone benefits.

One major research report entitled *The Contours and Consequences of Compassion at Work* (Lilius et al., 2008) looked at compassion in a healthcare (hospital) setting. The researchers found that compassion promoted commitment to the organisation. It was intriguing to note the following

> [...]compassion was reported as least frequent in units that perform direct patient care *as opposed to administrative or outpatient units, which runs counter to the intuition that those involved in the "business of care" would be more adept at or more likely to offer compassion and raises questions about how different organizational contexts might facilitate or inhibit the expression of compassion. Given what is known about the culture of occupational groups such as physicians and surgeons, where feeling rules demand resilience and self-reliance ...* it is perhaps unsurprising

that those in the medical/surgical units in our study reported less frequent compassion than others. *At the same time, previous research indicates that compassion can be found in unexpected contexts, such as a business school or a news agency ....* *It is also possible that* the lower frequency of compassion in the direct patient care units resulted from the "compassion burnout" commonly found in the helping professions .... *This suggests an intriguing avenue for future research that addresses the influence of occupational and organizational culture in the enactment of compassion at work.*

I was interested to read this as it mirrored my experience talking with humanitarian workers from global humanitarian organisations. I gave two talks on compassion and organisational change in Bangkok and Kuala Lumpur at a humanitarian conference in two successive years and on both occasions I had conversations with aid workers and employees of global charities who explained that they were too busy delivering aid, support and comfort to those in need to be able to find time to be compassionate to each other, that is, their co-workers. They admitted that the quality of their work and their ability to support people in disaster zones might actually be enhanced if, as co-workers, they were more compassionate towards each other. It seems that the nature of the work, and the bringing together of time-delimited teams of people (who work together for the duration of an emergency relief operation) means that there is precious little time to develop close interpersonal relationships, given that the work might be undertaken by people who might never meet each other again once the relief project has concluded. We see a similar phenomenon in healthcare too: I spoke at a healthcare conference in London on the subject of compassion and self-compassion and when I suggested that nurses ought to consider prioritising their own self-compassion and mental health in service of their patients, the suggestion resulted in tears from some nurses who said no one had ever said such a thing, at least not in public. Caring for yourself so that you can better care for others seems to be a simple premise that is hard to deliver on even though most people would agree with the logic and support it. This is why many people, me included, see compassion in the workplace, that is, the lack of it – as not just a failure of leadership from the top, but in fact a systemic failure which permeates everything.

DEVELOPING COMPASSION

There are some superb organisations and committed individuals around the world who are working tirelessly to promote the development of compassion in the workplace. Here is a snapshot of some of those places and people where compassion is taught, researched and explained.

In the United States

One of the leading centres for research into compassion and empathy is the Center for Compassion and Altruism Research and Education (CCARE) at Stanford. The Center was the idea of Dr James Doty, a Stanford neurosurgeon, entrepreneur and philanthropist. The development of the Center was accelerated by a visit from the Dalai Lama in 2007 and through a dialogue between the Dalai Lama and Stanford scientists, there was recognition of the enormous value to be gained through a better understanding of the connections between neuroscience and psychology, and Buddhism (as core to the contemplative traditions in world religion). Today the Center and its researchers continue to make a valuable contribution to the understanding of compassion in general but also in the workplace. Monica Worline and Jane Dutton, co-authors of *Awakening Compassion at Work*, are the founders of CompassionLab, which is a world leader in research collaboration around compassion in a work setting. Dr Daniel E. Martin is a scientist, also affiliated with CCARE at Stanford, whose research interests include the impact of individual difference and ideology on social corporate responsibility and human resources decision-making, together with the impact of ideology on compassion and psychological wellbeing. Dan has created a development and assessment platform which supports the development of compassion in the workplace.

On the other side of the country, we find the Center for Compassionate Leadership, which was founded by Laura Berland. The mission of the Center is to 'advance compassionate methods of leadership by integrating best practices of modern leadership, evidence-based science, and contemplative wisdom'. The Center does this through generating thought leadership, research, curriculum and training, community and collaboration. Another valuable resource for furthering compassion is Next Element, led by Dr Nate Regier, which provides a wealth of information on practical activities to strengthen compassion, self-compassion and empathy.

In Europe

Based at the Max Planck Institute in Berlin, Dr Tania Springer is a social neuroscientist and psychologist who researches the neuronal, hormonal, and developmental foundations of human social cognition. Tania and her colleagues Anne Böckler, Anita Tusche, and Peter Schmidt have done some extremely interesting work in the areas of compassion and empathy, including the creation of programmes which people can take to develop their compassion and empathy (through meditation and other training to enhance brain plasticity). As Dr Springer et al. (2018) mention:

> *Consistently, evidence from our lab and from within the ReSource Project revealed that expertise in compassion meditation and compassion training in novices is linked to enhanced positive affect, increased brain activity in regions associated with reward and affiliation that contain oxytocin receptors, and structural plasticity in brain areas involved in socio-affective processing.*

SELF-COMPASSION

An important dimension of compassion is the area of self-compassion, which is concerned with encouraging people to self-care and to undertake meditation and mindfulness as a way to build resilience and awareness. Self-compassion has nothing to do with spoiling or treating yourself. It is more about being gentle with 'you' and often involves a person actively forgiving themselves for past mistakes or current shortcomings. The thinking is that if you can get *self-compassion* going, one of the great outcomes is that you will be positioning yourself better to be able to be compassionate to others, in other words, to have the energy, drive and motivation to be of authentic service to others.

One of the world's leading scholars of self-compassion today is US-based Kristen Neff, PhD, who has this to say:

- Self-compassion is not self-pity.

- Self-compassion is not self-indulgence.

- Self-compassion is not self-esteem.

And she goes on to explain the difference between self-compassion and self-esteem:

> *In contrast to self-esteem, self-compassion is not based on self-evaluations. People feel compassion for themselves because all human beings deserve compassion and understanding, not because they possess some particular set of traits (pretty, smart, talented, and so on). This means that with self-compassion,* you don't have to feel better than others to feel good about yourself. *(Neff, 2003, pp. 85–10)*

'You don't have to feel better than others to feel good about yourself'. This is something that is hugely liberating for people today given the hyper-consumerist society we live in: it is also extremely powerful as a countermeasure to poor mental wellbeing brought on by feelings of a lack of self-worth.

DEVELOPING SELF-COMPASSION

The field of self-compassion is developing in leaps and bounds thanks to a number of talented individuals such as Kristen Neff and Brené Brown in the United States and Amanda Super in the United Kingdom.

Here's an example of what we can do in a practical sense to improve our self-compassion: the use of personal affirmation to replace self-criticism, with thanks to Catherine Moore (2019):

Personal affirmation

1. *I accept the best and worst aspects of who I am.*

2. *Changing is never simple but it's easier if I stop being hard on myself.*

3. *My mistakes just show that I'm growing and learning.*

4. *It's okay to make mistakes and forgive myself.*

5. *I am free to let go of others' judgments.*

6. *It's safe for me to show kindness to myself.*

7. *I deserve compassion, tenderness, and empathy from myself.*

8. *I release myself with forgiveness from today and move forward with self-love to tomorrow.*

9. *Every day is a new opportunity. I won't let self-doubt or judgment hold me back from the future.*

10. *I forgive myself and accept my flaws because nobody is perfect.*

11. *I'm not the first person to have felt this way, and I won't be the last, but I'm growing.*

Brené Brown has spoken extensively on vulnerability – her 2010 TEDx talk called *The Power of Vulnerability* is one of the top most-viewed TED talks of all time with over 30 million views. As Brené mentions:

'We don't have to do all of it alone. We were never meant to'.

So while we may attend to our self-compassion largely on our own, that doesn't mean we have to do everything on our own. It's always a good idea to ask for help.

In the United Kingdom, Amanda Super (2015) underscores the three main components of self-compassion:

• Being caring towards yourself.

• Recognising your connection to others.

• Learning to be mindful in the moment.

In my conversations with Amanda, I have been struck by the practical and warm manner in which Amanda advocates for more self-compassion. Amanda builds on the core constructs of Kristen Neff's approach to Self-Compassion, namely Self-Kindness, Common Humanity and Mindfulness through her programmes, blogs and foundational book.

So there are, as you can see, a variety of sources for you to explore with respect to both compassion and self-compassion. All that's left is to get started!

WHAT NEXT FOR COMPASSION?

Organisational Compassion

An organisational culture which supports compassionate ways of working is going to rely heavily on its senior leaders to set the tone. It's encouraging to be hearing more and more from organisations that are curious about embedding or even codifying compassionate working into organisational processes. Doing so can, I think, be tackled via a couple of routes at least – one of which is through determining purpose and values. The second is to consider this checklist for organisational compassion based on work by Dutton and others back in 2008, adapted by the author:

- *What is the scope of compassion the organisation envisages?* This is about the breadth of compassion extended by the organisation to the person or group who is suffering or in need of support.

- *What is the scale of the compassion that the organisation could offer?* This is about the volume of help that people might expect to receive i.e. how much assistance might be given to people who are suffering?

- *What is the speed of response that the organisation might be capable of achieving?* This is about how quickly the organisation responds to an individual in need.

- *What degree of specialisation is the organisation capable of in terms of delivering its compassionate support?* This is about the extent to which the organisation can tailor its response to the individual needs of the person or group in need of support (Dutton, Frost, et al., 2008).

- Adapted by the author.

Facilitating senior teams in a workshop setting, I have found that the desire and intention of leaders who 'get' compassionate ways of working are such that they want to see what can be done to 'bake compassion' into the DNA of the organisation. They realise fairly quickly that achieving such a goal can involve a pretty long journey as it will invariably require getting the buy-in of colleagues who are unconvinced and who think it would be better to put organisational effort elsewhere. Even in organisations which are generally very accepting of the concept of more care and more compassion, it is not always plain sailing. For example, a senior team (CEO, CFO, CHRO and others) on a compassion workshop together, shared that the organisation they worked for, a medium-sized hospitality group, had experienced caring for two colleagues who both happened to have been given a cancer diagnosis at around the same time. The firm rallied round, initially to change rotas and lighten the workload and then progressively to covering the job roles completely by deploying other employees, while keeping both people on full pay over a period of more than a year. One of the colleagues got through the cancer treatment but the other sadly did not make it. The group shared its feelings of deep sorrow for this, as they reminisced about the colleague who died, while also celebrating the fact that the other colleague was able to make a full return to work. They talked about how the firm's culture was very family-oriented and how they felt there was a high level of care prevalent in the company. They then mentioned that the two colleagues with the cancer diagnosis had both been with the firm for more than a decade. And as this thought came up, it made people wonder what the organisational response would have been if a newly arrived colleague with a tenure of just a couple of months – had suddenly received a cancer diagnosis. How might they react to that? Could they feel confident of responding with a similar level of support and compassion? Would it be something that as an organisation, they could be sure of happening in a predictable fashion, that is, as part of a codified, known, response? After much debate there was general consensus that this question might need to be put – at least temporarily – into the 'Too Difficult Box'. I surmised that sometimes, with events such as these – where we have colleagues suddenly given a serious ill-health diagnosis – the reaction of the people around them and of the organisation as an entity – is really very difficult to predict. The situational nature of the issue itself will make it hard to respond in a predictable way – and perhaps the answer, if there is one, is to be content with the notion that every occurrence of this nature has to be tailored to the unique situation and individual(s) involved. At the very least, however, there can be general codification of an organisational response, which has a recognised and predictable threshold for compassionate action. As you read this you may be thinking – wow – that hospitality group, what a fantastic organisation to be able to work for – and I would agree with you wholeheartedly. They have a great culture and at the same time, moral dilemmas to grapple with as well. It may be that the following approach (around 'collective noticing', 'collective feeling', and 'collective responding') might be useful in making sense of and resolving the paradoxes that can arise in the context of organisational compassion.

COLLECTIVE NOTICING, COLLECTIVE FEELING AND COLLECTIVE RESPONDING

In their paper, Compassion in Organizational Life, Kanov et al. outline three key ways to think about how compassion can be operationalised within an organisational context. These are collective noticing, collective feeling and collective responding:

> By propagating, legitimating [sic.], and coordinating members' acts in response to pain, an organization can increase its capacity for collective responding, and in turn the organizational compassion of the system. As with collective noticing and feeling, collective responding can produce a virtuous cycle in which members, through their actions, may highlight the need for and value of systems and policies, and reinforce a culture that supports the legitimation, propagation, and effective coordination of collective compassionate acts in the organization. (Kanov et al., 2004, pp. 808–827)

SOUNDS GREAT – BUT AT THE OTHER END OF THE COMPASSION CONTINUUM…

We have many examples of organisations that are at the other end of the continuum, such as those companies in logistics where employees are allegedly unable to go for regular toilet breaks out of fear of compromising their productivity targets and thereby losing their jobs. Or employees at call centres having deductions made to their wages for allegedly making too many trips to the rest-room – a result of the employer having asked the employees to drink plenty, so as to have clear throats when talking with customers! There is clearly a long way to go before we see more compassion in the workplace – and from these examples I think the key challenge is one around trust. In the absence of trust, organisations feel the need to monitor (increasingly it would seem, via various new technologies). And because of the creep in monitoring, so we see a corresponding erosion of trust. A cycle that looks hard to break for many companies.

STRENGTHENING ORGANISATIONAL COMPASSION

Here are some more ways in which organisational compassion can be built up and strengthened:

Through compassion training – sometimes known as virtuousness training – which can help to foster pro-social behaviour and motivation,

Fig. 7: Self-awareness/Self-compassion/Compassion.

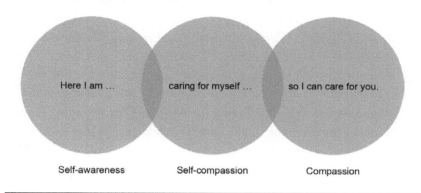

generate positive emotions and from a neuroscience perspective, impact areas of the brain associated with love and affiliation. Such programmes focus on self-awareness, self-compassion and compassion (Fig. 7).

Re-stating or revisiting values – ensuring that the organisation's values are appropriate for the future – *maybe using*:

Compassion circles – which can be run as self-standing events or as part of leadership programmes – focusing on appreciation and self-compassion. A compassion circle is a highly structured, one hour-long hosted and facilitated safe space in which participants can re-visit values, focus on self-compassion and reflect on inhibitors and enablers of compassion for others. Alternatively, one can hold regular team meetings where participants are encouraged not only to talk about the work but to share how they are feeling and how things are going for them. Other approaches to consider include inviting senior leaders to join *peer support groups* (e.g., a CEO peer group or a CHRO peer group) where they can share business and personal issues in a safe space.

Giving something back – organisational initiatives around volunteering in the community strengthen compassion and a sense of collegiate wellbeing.

Compassionate systems and processes – this is an emerging area in organisational life which shows great promise in terms of contributing to the development of compassionate organisations. Here is one example from Cisco Systems – which is also a good example of collective noticing, collective feeling and collective responding:

> *John Chambers, CEO, has a policy that he is to be notified (within 48 hours) of every instance in which a Cisco employee or an employee's*

immediate family member falls seriously ill or passes away. This policy increases individual members' vigilance by encouraging them to be on the look-out for pain: employees realize they need to be aware of a colleague's grief. The policy also expresses shared organizational values that indicate that people's family circumstances are legitimate foci of concern, thus making it more likely that members will share painful family news…. [this and other related policies] serve to legitimate and propagate organizational members' awareness of pain and their appreciation of its significance. In so doing they help to build the organization's capacity for collective noticing. (Kanov et al., 2004, pp. 808–827)

DEVELOPING YOUR OWN COMPASSION – QUESTIONS AS A LEADER THAT YOU CAN ASK YOURSELF

Here are some questions you can use when self-reflecting on your own level of compassion:

- Are you a secure base for your colleagues?
- How often do you talk about 'I/me' at the expense of 'We/us'?
- How often do your direct reports get individual time just with you?
- How often do you affirm and encourage your colleagues?
- Are you able to admit when you're wrong and apologise?
- What was the last courageous thing you did for the benefit of others?

Compassion is not a pink and fluffy concept. It has come into its own, now more than ever.

IN CONCLUSION

Here's a summary to illustrate why compassion is more important than ever for organisations of all types and sizes:

- Compassion promotes commitment to the organisation.
- Compassion breeds compassion.

- Compassion works both ways (giver and receiver).

- Compassion fosters more collaboration in the workplace.

- Compassion reduces staff turnover.

- Compassion fosters stronger bonds between co-workers.

- Compassion reduces the potential for burnout.

- Compassion can contribute to better mental health.

- Compassion creates the right conditions for innovation and creativity via safe spaces.

    Compassion is the radicalism of our time.

    Dalai Lama

8

EMPATHY IN THE WORKPLACE

EMPATHY – AN OVERVIEW

Empathy and compassion are closely related, and both are critical to the creation of more human workplaces and a more humane society. The reason why empathy is so important, particularly in an organisational context, is that it is linked to ethical decision-making and ethical leadership: ethical leadership is also linked to improved employee performance. In healthcare especially, empathy demonstrated towards patients leads to a range of positive health outcomes and improved patient and staff satisfaction – as we will find out during the course of this chapter.

Empathy has also been found to be a key skill for leaders in relation to intercultural communication; this is because when you can put yourself in the shoes of others, you can relate better to people from different cultures, with different backgrounds – and can, therefore, deliver more appropriate services. So where exactly did 'empathy' as a concept, come from?

Back in the eighteenth century Britain, it was 'sympathy', as a moral and aesthetic concept, which was keenly discussed by philosophers such as David Hume, Adam Smith, and Edmund Burke. The first appearance of 'empathy' was not until the early twentieth century, when it was initially used to describe an aesthetic experience (as in the feeling you get as you react to a beautiful landscape stretching out before you, or in describing a luxurious armchair or piece of furniture). As a relatively new word, 'empathy' is the best translation of the German word *Einfühlung* ('feeling-into') from which the English word originates. Given that German psychology greatly influenced American psychology from the late nineteenth century – thanks to German emigrés, who had trained in German labs coming to teach at American universities – empathy as a word quickly caught on in psychology circles. By 1913, 'empathy' had become the 'generally accepted translation of *Einfühlung*' (Lanzoni, 2018) and it has been part of the lexicon of psychology ever since. In recent years, it has become quite a fixture of management and leadership terminology – and for many people, especially in the business world, 'empathy' sounds more scientific that 'compassion'. For me, the two things are separate concepts, albeit related, that need to be seen as complementary ideas, but definitely not inter-changeable.

The reason for this distinction being made is that empathy is the required precursor to carrying out a compassionate act to alleviate someone else's suffering. It is something very special.

EMPATHY-FREE ZONES

We must be on our guard for 'empathy-free zones' in organisations. These are found in organisations where managers are singularly disinterested in anything other than meeting targets: they don't care at all about the people they manage – whether they are thriving or not, or whether they are in danger of burnout. If tightening the fiscal belt is required, these managers simply continue as if nothing has changed, pushing their people to achieve even more with even less. Whenever there is change in the organisation, these managers plough on ahead with no consultation with staff and no consideration of what the impact of any change might be on them. If any of their team members happens to suffer a life-changing event, empathy-free managers at best pay lip-service in terms of a human reaction. They certainly won't go out of their way to comfort their reports or to think of ways to help them during a personal crisis. For these managers, work is work and personal life is personal life – and personal issues should not be allowed to spill over into work time. Some of these empathy-free managers are themselves the victims of psychological damage: they might never have experienced or fully understood a truly empathic moment and they definitely won't want to reveal any of their own vulnerabilities, something which can invite empathy from their interlocutor. Paradoxically they might in fact merit our own expressions of empathy and compassion. A friend of mine, in pre-pandemic days, when asked by his empathy-free boss about how she managed to keep her team intact and happy, shared that after-work drinks (from time to time) was one way to enable people to relax, share stories, and to joke about work. The boss seemed genuinely intrigued by this approach to the extent that he announced that he might in fact try out this new strategy to manage and lead people himself. The problem of course is that after-work drinks are only meaningful and successful if you are already well on the way to building trust and collegiality. Such get-togethers need to be authentic. Going out for a meal or a drink with a boss who is only doing it for show – is one of the most awkward workplace experiences there is. I am sure you know what I mean!

THE DARK SIDE OF EMPATHY

Empathic Distress

In Chapter 7, we touched upon the phenomenon of 'distress tolerance' which is the ability to withstand hearing about or experiencing the suffering or distress of others. The issue of *empathic distress* is something that has been noticed and studied by neuroscientists (Singer & Klimecki, 2014) whereby empathic distress can be identified as one of a number of possible empathic reactions people can experience upon learning of the pain of another. What happens is that if a person sees another person in pain they find themselves actually physically experiencing discomfort – or even pain akin to that being felt by the other person. The phenomenon has been noticed in those who are occupied in customer facing and 'helping' jobs: the person can *feel* with the other person and take upon themselves painful emotions to the extent that they themselves start to experience these extremely disturbing emotions. This can result in tremendous distress and has the potential to lead to a breakdown or burn-out. This is why some people – who are not as empathic – can sometimes be genuinely non-plussed by what they see as an over-reaction by a person hearing bad news affecting a third person. The reality of the matter is that we are all unique and will react in different ways depending on a variety of factors including the degree of closeness to the people involved.

Empathy Decline

There have been a number of studies over the years which look at the empathy levels of people involved in the care sector such as nurses and doctors. Different studies have come up with different and sometimes inconclusive results, although there does seem to be general agreement that capacity for empathy is adversely affected (perhaps not surprisingly) by factors such as overload, lack of resources, and people being stretched to breaking point. Some studies have found evidence for this, that is, that it is more difficult to show empathy when there is role overload (Dutton et al., 2014).

Of more concern might be the decline – in a general sense – of empathy *overall*. In a 2010 article entitled: "The End of Empathy?" by Sara Konrath PhD of The Empathy Gap, Sara suggested that even while data she had gathered indicated that empathy might be in decline, she doubted that it was dead. She and her team had run an analysis of around 14,000 university students to compare empathy levels between 2000 and 2010. In her words:

> The good news is that empathy is not 'destroyed' or 'under siege' [as reported in a Fox News blog] …… Instead, empathy may be sick. Not 'you have 6 months to live' sick, more like 'you need to spend a few days in bed' sick. In other words, although there has been a decline in empathy, there are a few key things to consider about the data before declaring a state of emergency on the moral health of the nation [the United States]. Konrath (2010)

Accordingly to Sara, overall empathy levels were still in the mid-range (on a 1–5 scale) despite the decline, so we are not in the business of stating that a generation of college students are completely devoid of empathy. Empathy is present although the prognosis for an improvement in 2010 did not seem encouraging at all, given that Sara's doctoral work showed an upward trend in the prevalence of narcissism as a behavioural trait. Empathy down, narcissism up. Other research reports according to Sara, point to the same pattern. She concludes:

> If recent trends continue, this could eventually translate into broader societal problems. I'm most concerned that current declines in empathy could lead to negative reciprocal spirals as people feed off of each other's low empathy.

That was the situation 10 years ago. So what is the situation now? Well, given the tumultuous events of recent years and the polarisation of society in many parts of the world, one can only surmise that the disruptive situation we face on a number of fronts – is not stacking up in favour of empathy. That said, if there is a silver lining in all the grim news of recent years, I think it would be to recognise the empathic outpouring of support and heartfelt recognition of the health services across the globe as well as the empathic surge of anti-racist sentiment in the aftermath of the tragic death of George Floyd. If we were being optimistic, we might say that there have been significant examples of empathy in action, which is to be welcomed. But at the same time there is no doubt that we still have a huge mountain to climb.

In their State of Workplace Empathy 2020 Special Report entitled *Workplace Empathy: What Leaders Don't Know Can Hurt Them*, the benefits management solution provider Businessolver pointed out that 'Empathy's value in the workplace has risen in recent years, but progress has stalled'. The Businessolver report goes on to say that 'a significant disconnect persists between how executives view workplace empathy and how employees experience it'. Here's some data to consider:

- Only 48% of employees believe companies as a whole are empathetic, versus 86% of CEOs.

- 91% of CEOs say their company is empathetic, but only 68% of employees agree.

- Only 45% of employees view CEOs in general as empathetic, versus 87% of CEOs; 63% of employees say their own CEOs are empathetic.

I think this belies a common thread in many polls that compare CEO perceptions of their organisation with that of their employees. It's regrettable to have to say it but it's not often we find alignment of perception with reality among CEOs and their people! (For example, at an individual CEO level it is not surprising to find CEOs rating themselves (on a typical 360-degree feedback assessment) as 'excellent listeners' – maybe self-scoring a 9/10. And yet reports consistently rate their bosses in the 5–6 range. Maybe CEOs are out of touch because they aren't listening or listening hard enough.)

In the *What Leaders Don't Know Can Hurt Them* report, 68% of CEOs believe companies are generally empathetic. Only 48% of employees do.

EMPATHY IN COMPANIES

The situation regarding the health of empathy globally – is pretty fluid we might say, which is something borne out by the results of a 2016 poll – which

Table 9:   The Top 20 Most Empathetic Companies 2016.

No.	Company	Sector	Score (Out of 100)
1	Facebook	Technology	100
2	Alphabet (Google)	Technology	99.4
3	LinkedIn	Technology	98.8
4	Netflix	Technology	98.2
5	Unilever	Consumer Goods	97.7
6	Southwest Airlines	Travel and Tourism	97.1
7	Microsoft	Technology	96.5
8	Whole Foods Market	Consumer Goods	95.9
9	Johnson & Johnson	Pharma	95.3
10	SAP SE	Technology	94.7

Adapted from Belinda Parmar: *The Top 20 Most Empathetic Companies 2016*, Harvard Business Review, 1 December 2016.

looked at which companies are the most empathetic – and what has happened in the four short years since then. The top 10 companies for empathy in 2016 (based on an analysis of the internal culture, CEO performance, ethics and social media presence) are shown in Table 9.

In the intervening years since this report was produced, a lot has happened to the various companies listed. Their fortunes have waxed and waned; CEO reputations in one or two cases have suffered a few knocks. My own work looking at the emotional intelligence of organisations suggests that company reputation is a fragile thing and the one major factor which impacts such ratings is the performance of the CEO. If the CEO is not widely regarded as having empathy, then it is highly unlikely that the company will exhibit much of it.

Let's now take a look at Glassdoor ratings of companies for 2020 (Glassdoor uses reviews by current and former employees). The first thing to notice is how only one of the companies in Table 9 features in Table 10.

We will examine in due course what it is that might make some companies more empathetic than others. What is it that the most empathetic actually *do*?

Table 10: Glassdoor Ratings for 2020.

No.	Company	Sector	Rating Out of 5
1	Hub Spot	Software	4.6
2	Bain & Co	Consulting	4.6
3	DocuSign	Electronic Documents	4.6
4	In-N-Out Burger	Food and Beverage	4.6
5	Sammons Financial Group Companies	Financial Services	4.5
6	Lawrence Livermore National Laboratory	Federal Research Facility	4.5
7	Intuitive Surgical	Medical Robotics	4.5
8	Ultimate Software	Consumer Goods	4.5
9	VIPKid	Online Education	4.5
10	Southwest Airlines	Travel and Tourism	4.5

Notes: While they don't make the top 10, Google and LinkedIn place at #11 (4.5) and #12 (4.5), respectively. Facebook is at #23 (4.4). Only Southwest Airlines makes it into the top 10 in both lists. Adapted from https://www.glassdoor.com/Award/Best-Places-to-Work-LST_KQ0,19.htm

DEVELOPING EMPATHY IN COMPANIES

In 2014, James W. Quigley, the CEO of GoCanvas, which provides mobile apps and forms for data collection and sharing, penned an interesting set of notes entitled: "Why Every Business Needs a Culture of Empathy." After six years developing the business, James had this to say about building empathic capability in the company:

How do you strengthen your company's empathy muscle?

- *Transparency is key*: 'Empathy doesn't happen in a vacuum: to understand someone, you need to connect to their authentic self'.

- *An opportunity to give back*: Through the AnteUp* programme, 'We wanted to give people the opportunity to give back in areas that they were passionate about and connect with people outside of their day-day work. '(*AnteUp involves gifting the GoCanvas solution to external projects that GoCanvas staffers are passionate about).

- *Driving innovation*: 'We think a deeper ability to be empathetic is key to product innovation, improved sales, the most authentic marketing … and empathy helps us continue to innovate by anticipating customer needs'.

- *It starts at the top*: 'I have made sure that our culture of empathy starts with me and then is rooted in how all of our team leads and members approach achieving their goals. We hire team members and team leads considering their ability to be empathetic and we have taken that as far as curating investors and board members who are equally committed to our culture of empathy'.

The GoCanvas story provides us with a useful mini-case study of empathy in action. And the importance of empathy in business was more recently underscored by Apple CEO Tim Cook:

> *People will try to convince you that you should keep empathy out of your career. Don't accept this false premise. Tim Cook, CEO of Apple in his 2017 MIT commencement address.*
>
> *At the time of Tim's remarks, 20% of US employers offered empathy training for their managers and in a recent survey of 150 CEOs, over 80% recognised empathy as key to success. Jamil Zaki: Making Empathy Central to Your Company Culture, Harvard Business Review, 30 May 2019*

So why should people – and CEOs in particular – pay more attention to empathy and try to better appreciate the impact that it has? Unfortunately, senior leaders often underestimate 'intangibles', or they fail to appreciate the impact that a lack of empathy has on short-, medium-, and long-term business success (and sustainability). According to Businessolver, the vast majority of employees today see empathy as 'a key driver of their productivity'. In fact 76% of them do. But only 52% of CEOs see the connection. Employees also see high levels of empathy as a critical lever to drive down staff turnover (70% of employees). But only 40% of CEOs hold the same view. Astonishingly, a whopping 82% of CEOs were happy to go along with the idea that a company's financial performance is tied to empathy – but as we've seen, only just over 50% of them see empathy as having anything to do with motivation and productivity. This is almost a contradiction in terms!

EMPATHIC BIAS

Empathy is a powerful and underutilised human attribute. At the same time, we must also be aware of the bias inherent in empathy. The psychologist Paul Bloom in his book *Against Empathy* – has done a great job of exploring how we humans are innately susceptible to bias when it comes to experiencing empathy. Put simply, we have a bias towards feeling empathy towards people who are more like us. Susan Lencioni in her book *Empathy* explains:

> *Today, neuroscientists call it 'parochial empathy' and find that it can be mitigated when subjects listen to narrative descriptions of individuals from social and ethnic groups unfamiliar to them. Susan Lencioni referencing Emile G. Bruneau, Mina Cikara, and Rebecca Saxe (2015).*

The challenge lies in creating the environment for people to want to listen or hear about others who are not like them.

As human beings we tend to identify more with singular instances of tragedy or loss of life, than with terrible events that happen on a grand scale. A missing child in our immediate neighbourhood is more likely to attract concern and attention at a deep level – than news stories of many children dying in faraway, war-torn lands. It is not that we cannot feel empathy for those who live on the other side of the world, but it is harder for us to do so when we don't have the depth of familiarity with those environments. It is also harder to make sense of tragedies that happen on a huge scale: we feel sadness, but we may not be able to *truly* empathise. That is, until the tragedy starts to get closer to home.

Despite empathy being vulnerable to bias, there is still a great deal we can derive as individuals and workers from developing our own capacity for empathy and empathetic behaviour.

DEVELOPING EMPATHY IN INDIVIDUALS

The Stanford neuroscientist Jamil Zaki has made a great contribution to the understanding of empathy in human society. In 2019, he was interviewed by Emma Seppälä of the Stanford Center for Compassion and Altruism Research and Education who asked him why empathy in society might be declining. Here's what Jamil had to say:

> *People empathize most easily when they can see others' suffering with their own eyes, or when their actions are visible to others. But*

the modern world has stripped them away. Humans increasingly live in cities and alone. We see more people than ever but know fewer of them. Rituals that used to bring us into regular contact, ranging from bowling leagues to grocery shopping, have been replaced by more solitary pursuits, often carried out online. The result is our interactions with each other are thinned out, anonymous and tribal – barren soil for empathy. Emma Seppälä, 11 June 2019, Washington Post

So our task is to ensure that we find or create fertile soil for empathy. And organisations can take an active role in facilitating this through the following actions, as suggested by the 2020 Special Report: *Workplace Empathy: What Leaders Don't Know Can Hurt Them,* adapted and added to by the author (Table 11).

In addition to the eight actions suggested in Table 11, there are many other valuable activities that people can undertake to increase their empathy levels.

Examples of these include:

Meditation

A small study by Emory University entitled: *Compassion meditation enhances empathic accuracy and related neural activity* by Jennifer S. Mascaro, James K. Rilling, Lobsang Tenzin Negi, and Charles L. Raison (2013) describes how:

> *Twenty-one healthy participants received functional MRI scans while completing an empathic accuracy task, the Reading the Mind in the Eyes Test (RMET), both prior to and after the completion of either CBCT [cognitive-based compassion training] or a health discussion control group. Upon completion of the study interventions, participants randomized to CBCT were significantly more likely than control subjects to have increased scores on the RMET and increased neural activity in the inferior frontal gyrus (IFG) and dorsomedial prefrontal cortex (dmPFC) [areas in the brain known to accommodate empathic activity]. Moreover, changes in dmPFC and IFG activity from baseline to the post-intervention assessment were associated with changes in empathic accuracy. These findings suggest that CBCT may hold promise as a behavioural intervention for enhancing empathic accuracy and the neurobiology supporting it.*

Table 11. Eight Key Actions to Promote Empathy in Organisations.

Action	Report Details; Author Additions	Author Comments
1 Develop policies and practices that open lines of communication directly to leadership	Employees are asking for 'face-to-face' time with leadership, and executives need to create these opportunities to listen to employees' concerns, including in a virtual format during periods of distancing and in remote work environments	CHROs can take the lead in making this happen, supported by the CEO. They can actively influence erstwhile prescriptive directives and rules by 'humanising'communication about them and inculcating an open and friendly, 'if you aren't sure, contact me' approach
2 Consider cross-generational leadership training, as more employees today believe that empathy can be learned	Employees at different life stages experience unique challenges in the current strained and uncertain work environment. Learned empathy across generations can boost productivity and employees' overall perception of their workplace. In the recent survey, 73% of employees said that empathy can be learned, up from 65% in 2017	Baby boomer CEOs may represent the last bastion of old-style thinking on empathy and how to develop trust among employees. Younger generations coming up through the ranks see things differently and actively want to change what was often referred to as 'the psychological contract'. Try to avoid 'doing things to people' – instead, involve them upstream so that they feel heard, that their influence counts and that they feel respected
3 Explore benefits, clarify policies and encourage behaviours that promote work–life flexibility	Today a successful company culture needs to reflect employees' need to honour their lives and families outside of work. Flexibility is highly and frequently cited by employees as contributing to better overall mental wellbeing. Although some benefits could be falling short, employees may also misperceive offerings such as comp time that are often vague and frequently misunderstood. CEOs can help bridge the gap between policy and culture to ensure that benefits meet the needs of the whole individual	Trust and clarity lie at the root of success for this kind of initiative. There are business cultures around the world that for decades have insisted that it is necessary for bosses to see and observe their teams working – right here, in a physical sense. The disruption to this way of thinking is now plain for all to see and it is up to the CEO, the CHRO and all members of the management team to chip away at the old edifice of presenteeism and help to strengthen, not undermine, the new culture of dialled-up trust demanded by the shift for many workers to WFH (Work From Home)

Table 11. (Continued)

Action	Report Details; Author Additions	Author Comments
4 Empower change agents across the organisation	CEOs and employees are divided on who is responsible for improving workplace empathy. On average, employees look to their managers as drivers of empathy. CEOs must set the tone for empathy from the top and encourage managers to carry that message throughout the organisation. With many working remotely or in high-stress roles, it is up to CEOs to model empathetic actions for managers across the leadership spectrum	While CEOs should take the lead in empowering change agents, we also need the CHRO and the human resources function to get right behind any such initiatives. Whenever there is energy to revisit purpose and values, people should see this as a golden opportunity to actively challenge some of the motherhood and apple pie statements that companies habitually make around values – and challenge the organisation to embrace empathy and compassion in an honest and authentic way, describing clearly what empathy and compassion look like in real-life, and moving away from almost meaningless 'also ran' values that so many organisations lazily put in place to 'get the values job done'
5 Support employee mental health	Nobody has cracked the code on de-stigmatising mental health. Employees and CEOs alike agree that organisations should be doing more yet both groups fear they will be viewed as a burden for coming forward with issues. Reflections and honest conversations coming from the top can begin to dismantle stigma and deepen empathy throughout the organisation	Improving mental wellbeing is definitely a work in progress even for the most enlightened of companies across the globe. It is a fine and nuanced thing: I know that more and more people are finding it easier to talk about depressive periods (more than just feeling 'a bit low') but they stop short of being able to fully embrace the idea of working with someone who has a (controlled) condition that people are scared of, because they don't understand enough about it. Such as schizophrenia. Slow progress is being made though

6	Make empathy something you talk about in public	Companies need to champion their commitment to empathy through social media and the normal company descriptors (websites, annual reports, etc.)	CEOs should look for metrics to attempt to measure positive changes that can be related to empathy initiatives. The CEO also needs to convince the Board to support this line and get them to hold the management team and the CEO accountable to achieve what they set out to do
7	Create empathy stories and spread them internally	Stories that bring empathy to life can be promulgated through company newsletters and celebrated in individual employee reviews	Performance reviews should include stories and recollections about empathic acts and sharing of what employees have done to help their team mates and how they've contributed to the creation of a more human workplace
8	Consider how to imbue regular meetings and check-ins with a more empathic style and approach	Rather than jumping straight into a meeting (either offline or online), take some time to check in with people, hear their news, what they are doing outside of work	Such check-ins do not have to eat into valuable discussion time – in fact, they are worth the effort to allow people to get focused relaxed and better able to think clearly and effectively. There is an Asian maxim claimed by the Chinese, Japanese, Koreans and others that says: *Go Slow to Go Fast*. Worth bearing in mind!

Based on and adapted from: State of Workplace Empathy 2020 Special Report entitled Workplace Empathy: *What Leaders Don't Know Can Hurt Them* with author additions and comments.

- *Note: The* Reading the Mind in the Eyes Test *(RMET) involves looking at black-and-white photographs of different facial expressions – except that the photographs only show the eye region of the face. People taking the test are then asked to say what kind of emotion or thinking is being invoked in each expression.*

Mindfulness is a hugely popular activity and has helped many people in a variety of ways.

Reading fiction

In her 2019 article for *BBC Psychology*, Claudia Hammond examines whether reading fiction can help people to develop their empathy and compassion. There is general agreement that reading fiction and accessing characters who are very different from us – is a great way to gain perspective on how others think, act and behave. Claudia references the work of the Canadian cognitive psychologist Keith Oatley who suggests reading fiction could be called 'The Mind's Flight Simulator' as it affords the reader the chance to immerse themselves in other behaviours and to learn (vicariously) about the beliefs and mores of others – a chance to mentally 'try things on for size'. In another example Claudia mentions how Dutch researchers asked university students to read the first chapter from Nobel Prize winner Jose Saramago's novel *Blindness*, in which a man is waiting in his car at traffic lights when suddenly he goes blind. A passer-by offers to drive his car home for him and ends up stealing it. When the students read about the man's experience their empathy levels immediately started to rise and – if they had been emotionally touched by the story – a week later they scored even higher on empathy than they did immediately after reading the story. Claudia concludes:

So the research shows that perhaps reading fiction does make people behave better. Certainly, some institutions consider the effects of reading to be so significant that they now include modules on literature. At the University of California Irvine, for example, Johanna Shapiro from the Department of Family Medicine firmly believes that reading fiction results in better doctors and has led the establishment of a humanities programme to train medical students.

It looks as though it's time to lose the stereotype of the shy bookworm whose nose is always in a book because they find it difficult to deal with other people. In fact, these bookworms might be better than anyone else at understanding human beings.

Claudia Hammond, BBC Psychology, Does Reading Fiction Make Us Better People? Posted on 3 June 2019

Groups, associations, and volunteering

There are many ways in which we can create the foundation for working on our empathy. Joining a club, association or community group has always been a great way for people to get together and enjoy each other's company, although this route to market for increasing empathy has been somewhat compromised by the need for social distancing during the global health crisis. That said, the resourcefulness of people has meant we have been able to find digital alternatives (though it's not quite the same I would say). There are also charitable organisations that help support people and even one called The Empathy Club which exists to promote more empathy in society across the world. Volunteering is another great way to help out and do good.

Nurturing Curiosity

In his April 2020 article in the *Harvard Business Review*, "Empathy Starts with Curiosity," Peter Brennan makes an excellent point about listening with curiosity – and humility – as the pathway to developing empathy:

> [...]before demonstrating my understanding, I have to develop it. I need to ask questions and be open and listen and learn. Which takes humility. Humility is not knowing. And that, eventually and almost always, leads to empathy which leads to compassion.
> Peter Brennan, Empathy Starts With Curiosity, April 2020, Harvard Business Review

And in a conversation with Dr Robyn Wilson, CEO of Praxis Management Consulting, about curiosity and empathy, Robyn had this to share:

> Leaders frequently get feedback about their perceived inability to empathise – whether it be during leadership development programmes, 360 assessments or annual reviews. This is often a source of frustration for them because some find it hard to get their head around how empathy actually works, let alone how best to develop themselves to be more empathetic. In various coaching conversations with CEOs and other senior leaders, I've often suggested that they approach things differently – and start from a place of curiosity. Having curiosity about others helps a leader to be more open to other people and

their situations. It can draw them towards these people. This is the opposite to taking a more removed, judgmental approach as leaders attempt to try to work out what's gone wrong in a given situation.

So leaders can be curious about what they see and hear when they are observing other people's behaviour. It could be about figuring out what's happening for someone in their world, or simply about reflecting back something someone shares that has caught their attention, for example. The beauty of curiosity is that it flows from a place of finding questions and not from a place of judgment – because that is where curiosity dies. A well-asked, thoughtful open question – while showing genuine interest in the person and their answer – is a great step in the right direction and touches empathy. And ultimately, being curious about the story the other person may be telling themselves given their context, their feelings, their concerns, their hopes and fears – leads you towards empathy.

Leadership is about looking after the people who look after the results. This means that it is incumbent on leaders to find ways of caring and supporting that work best for their people. Empathy informs and monitors this work of a leader.

In Chapter 9, we will take a closer look at what kind of questions and style of questioning we can use to develop empathetic listening and compassionate actions. These include: Appreciative Inquiry, the role of questioning in making sense of complex systems and in addressing Wicked Problems, questions to establish what kind of context we are operating in as a way to inform what actions we might take, plus Socratic questioning, MI (Motivational Interviewing) and the importance of storytelling (given that stories are often built around rhetorical questions).

EMPATHY, GENDER, PERSPECTIVE-TAKING, DEVELOPING CULTURAL SYNERGY, AND LEADERSHIP – THE IMPORTANCE OF AUTHENTICITY

I would like to conclude this chapter with a brief look at how empathy, gender, perspective-taking, developing cultural synergy, and leadership are connected – and how in all of this, authenticity is critical.

In this time of disruption on many fronts, we look to our leaders for guidance, inspiration and comfort. We want to be able to follow those who are ethical and trustworthy. At this time, these things (ethical behaviour and trust) seem to be in short supply, right across the world.

Gender

Something we need to strive to have more of – is empathy for *everyone* on the gender spectrum. We must also avoid characterising empathy as being a 'female' or 'male' thing and look for empathy from all – including our political and corporate leaders.

The psychologist Cordelia Fine pointed out in her 2010 book *Delusions of Gender: How Our Minds, Society and Neurosexism Create Difference* (New York: W.W. Norton) that advocating the idea that 'men systematise, women empathise' was really not very helpful – a theme supported by Margery Lucas in her work about Fine and her thinking.. In my view then, when it comes to empathy, we should hold male and female leaders to the same high standards. And this is where we also find a connection via empathy to ethical behaviour and ethical leadership.

Perspective-taking

In a 2013 article in *The Guardian* entitled *Barack Obama and the 'empathy deficit'*, the journalist Mark Honigsbaum wrote an excellent piece on empathy and asked what might be at the root of empathy development. He says that *perspective-taking* is key (**I have rendered the key words in bold**):

> [...]*when we make the imaginative effort to step into the shoes of another person and* **see things from their perspective,** *we become less capable of ignoring their suffering. Indeed, brain imaging studies of Buddhists who use meditation exercises to contemplate compassion on a daily basis show increased activation of the amygdala and other parts of the brain's empathy circuit.*

He goes on to say:

> *The evidence suggests, in fact that the best way to weaken people's racial or other biases is through frank, empathic dialogue ... Given*

that, **the best approach to combating racism and sexism may be empathy.** *Mark Honigsbaum: Barack Obama and the 'empathy deficit',* The Guardian, *4 January 2013*

Perspective-taking is also essential for building *cultural synergy* – a concept devised by the organisation behaviour professor and thought-leader Nancy J. Adler – and for developing better understanding between different kinds of groups overall.

Perspective-taking and Cultural Synergy

In a blog about developing cultural synergy, Joyce Jenkins (2020) explains the following:

> *In the business, intercultural and human resource management fields, Adler's concept of 'cultural synergy' is often referred to. When employing cultural synergy, different cultural perspectives are acknowledged and new alternatives created which combine the approaches and ideas of the cultures involved, creating something which is better than the sum of its parts – thus, 'synergy.'*
>
> *Under this heading is the specific competence of 'creating new alternatives'. Someone (who is skilled at this) will typically want to understand issues from different viewpoints, enabling group members from different backgrounds to use their different approaches to find creative solutions (which may be new and different from the proposals of any of the individual approaches) to the issues they have to deal with.*

Creating cultural synergy, therefore, is a key competence for leaders in many contexts – and deploying ACE attributes to achieve this – can be highly effective and benefit all concerned.

Authenticity and Leadership

Authentic displays of empathy engender trust.

When it comes to politicians, however, we tend to regard shows of emotion with a certain degree of scepticism – which is why we have grown wary of politicians kissing babies while on walkabouts (hopefully this is quickly on its way to becoming a thing of the past). How we view them clearly depends on the politician in question – and how much trust they have been able to bank with the general public over time. I found it interesting that as far back as 2013, Mark Honigsbaum suggested that the old adage 'It's the Economy, stupid' – as being the key to winning an election – might need the 'E' changing – to 'Empathy'. At the time of the US Presidential Election, Mitt Romney sensed this and in the closing stages of his campaign tried to paint himself as being equally compassionate as Barack Obama. But by then it was too late.

People can tell when empathy or compassion is genuine or not.

And finally here's Jacinda Ardern, Prime Minister of New Zealand, on how it takes courage and strength to be empathetic and compassionate:

> *I've made a very deliberate decision, that in the Westminster type of politics we have here in New Zealand, which is very adversarial, that there is still a place for us to push back a little on that … I've always said that it takes courage and strength to be empathetic and I'm very proudly an empathetic, compassionately-driven politician.*
>
> *-Jacinda Ardern, interview with the BBC, 14 November 2018.*

It's great to see compassion and empathy taking centre-stage in this way.

PART THREE

WHAT HAPPENS NEXT?

9

WHAT DO WE NEED TO STOP, START, OR CONTINUE?

- Appreciative Inquiry and asking questions to practice ACE.

- Practicing the ACE approach.

- Being altruistic.

- Being compassionate.

- Being empathic.

- Three mini-case studies to illustrate ACE in action in organisations.

- Critical leadership skills for a disrupted world.

APPRECIATIVE INQUIRY AND ASKING QUESTIONS AS A WAY TO PRACTICE ALTRUISM, COMPASSION, AND EMPATHY

Appreciative Inquiry (AI) is useful way of exploring new ways of doing things. It has been deployed successfully in organisations for many years. As an approach, it takes as its starting point asking what's working well, celebrating successes to date, and thinking about how to build on the strengths that a team or organisation already has. In its early incarnation, AI was a four-stage process consisting of 'Discover'; 'Dream'; 'Design', and 'Deliver' or 'Destiny'. A fifth stage 'Define' – put in at the beginning – has now become part of the approach.

Define – What is it that we want to concentrate on?

Discover – Through dialogue, finding out what works, what's been successful so far.

Dream – What could 'be'? This is about imagining new possibilities.

Design – Figuring out the best possible next step.

Deliver – Arriving at a way to conduct the next possible best step. 'Destiny' is often used as a term for this stage.

AI is a useful tool to enable us to make progress. At the same time, it may also have its limitations, given the sheer pace of change and disruption that we are experiencing in the world today. But it's a reasonable place to start. We can overlay altruism, compassion, and empathy in order to strengthen AI and enable our exploration of what it will take to create more human workplaces.

In addition to AI, the *Stop–Start–Continue* approach, borrowed from the field of organisational development, is also a tried and tested way of enabling groups to define what to prioritise in terms of future steps. We want to continue doing good and effective things, sort out those things that aren't serving us very well anymore and drop them – and, at the same time of course, bring in new ideas and innovations. *Stop–Start–Continue* can be a small or large group exercise which involves rotating people through a series of conversations (either in person, capturing ideas and views on flipcharts) or virtually, using any number of virtual whiteboard tools that are available to us now and then comparing results across the three categories to decide what is best to tackle first. Actions to take in service of humanising the workforce could potentially take many forms and if we are not careful, result in us trying to 'boil the ocean'. So applying Stop, Start, and Continue principles can help us to ensure we are not biting off more than we can chew.

There are other valuable and highly pragmatic approaches we can take to try to make sense of the complexity of our disruptive times. The Human System Dynamics Institute (HSD) based in the United States and founded by Glenda Eoyang uses a frame which enables us to engage with complexity, find a way through and advance. The Institute's approach is to ask *What? So What? Now What?* as a pathway to Adaptive Action – to taking the Next Wise Action:

> *HSD is grounded in inquiry. Answers have short shelf lives in complex systems, and a good question can last a lifetime. Adaptive Action is three key questions [What? So What? Now What?] to keep you*

moving forward. From Human Systems Dynamics Institute, website:
https://www.hsdinstitute.org/what-is-hsd/inquiry-based.html

Cognitive Edge, also US-based, has developed the Cynefin framework which helps people to figure out their real context so that they can make better decisions through assessing whether the context is obvious, complicated, complex, or chaotic. Determining this helps to determine the nature of the response.

So the key thing for me is the business of asking questions and how we can bring the ACE approach (Altruism, Compassion, and Empathy) to bear on challenges caused by the great disruptions of the day by asking the right questions in the right kind of way – appropriate to the people and to the situation at hand.

Another useful thing to do is to consider the contribution that Socratic questioning can make. *Socratic questioning* is a way of asking questions created by the great Greek philosopher Socrates. His idea was to enable his students to test the truth of the subject in question – a process which often results in answers that are quite different to what you might have imagined them to be. Socratic questioning is used often in psychology and coaching – and is frequently deployed to try to solve problems.

Here are some examples of Socratic questioning:

- Why do you say that?

- How is this related?

- Could you explain this in more detail?

→ *These are questions that help to clarify things.*

- What can we assume from this?

- What does that mean?

- Can you verify your assumption?

→ *These can help to produce the assumptions we need to make in order to move forward.*

- Do you have an example of this in real life?

- What has caused you to believe this?

- Why do you think this happened?

→ *These are questions that elicit evidence.*

- Is there another way to look at this?

- Have you thought of the other person's point of view?

- Who benefits and who loses from this consequence?

→ *These questions help us with perspective-taking: they will often require empathy too.*

- What is the implication of this?

- Does this relate to previous knowledge?

- How does X affect Y?

→ *These questions allow us to ascertain consequences.*

- What does this mean?

- How can you apply this in your everyday life?

- What was the point of this inquiry?

→ *These are questions that help us to 'question the question'.*

Another approach we can consider is *Motivational Interviewing* (MI) which can be applied primarily in one-to-one situations. This uses a form of questioning (it started with counsellors helping people to deal with substance abuse issues) to enable the person to take control of their actions in order to assist them in getting through severe personal challenges. MI uses a guiding style to engage people (often clients or patients that is), to clarify their strengths and aspirations, and to evoke their own motivations for change and promote autonomy in decision-making (Rollnick, Miller, & Butler, 2008).

MI relies on some assumptions:

- How we speak to people is likely to be just as important as what we say.

- Being listened to and understood is an important part of any change.

- The person who has the problem is the person who has the answer to solving it.

- People only change their behaviour when they feel ready – not when they are told to do so.

- The solutions that people find for themselves are the most enduring and effective

   (Rollnick et al., 2008).

I think MI has the potential to be very useful in conversations in the workplace where we are trying to be more compassionate and empathic. Situationally, the *tone and timbre* of the questioning style in MI may be more appropriate than the Socratic method, especially when the topic of conversation is highly personal or emotional for the discussants. MI is altruistic: you are helping the person to help themselves. The need or necessity for you to benefit personally doesn't feature. An exception might be when you are trying to help a close relative or close friend to get through a difficult time in their lives: if they are happier and more able to cope, it is likely that your stress levels will reduce accordingly, at least to a certain degree.

There are four general principles in MI ('RULE'). Here they are:

R – resist the urge to change the individual's course of action through didactic means.

U – understand it's the individual's reasons for change, not those of the interlocutor, that will elicit a change in behaviour.

L – listening is important because the solutions lie with the individual, not the interlocutor.

E – empower the individual to understand that they have the ability to change their behaviour (Rollnick et al., 2008).

MI is not about offering direct advice or prescribing solutions without the person's permission or without actively encouraging the person to make their own choices. In a clinical setting, patients exposed to MI are more likely to enter, stay in and complete their treatment programme and take part in follow up meetings. I was intrigued by the approach taken by MI because it struck me as being a warm and human way of interacting. It's a compassionate way of relating, especially when it comes to having difficult conversations. MI opens up the possibility of a different, more empathic type of dialogue.

Storytelling can also be a rich resource when it comes to exploration of ideas, asking questions, and seeking answers. As a topic, storytelling is an important component in many leadership development programmes and there are individuals and organisations around the world ready to help people to become better and more effective storytellers and through this, to connect more intimately with people, especially if they are leaders, with the people who follow them. A fascinating branch of storytelling is *digital storytelling* which has been pioneered in the United Kingdom by Patient Voices. Patient Voices runs workshops that enable healthcare professionals, carers, and patients to develop their own stories and narratives. The outcome is both cathartic for the storytellers and also reassuring, in many cases, to those people who might be experiencing similar health-related challenges. I have worked with Patient Voices on developing staff stories (with staff from within my own organisation) as a way of illustrating institutional values and showcasing compassion in particular. Such stories are encouraging for staff to watch and for newcomers to the organisation, the invitation to listen to a couple of digital stories is a great way to give people a sense of the kind of organisation they have joined – from a very human perspective. In fact, we also encouraged people who were *thinking* of joining us to look at the stories and reflect on whether what they saw and heard, resonated with them. The promotion and showcasing of staff stories, whether digital or otherwise, can be used to great effect in both talent attraction and talent retention. The key thing is that such digital stories must come across as authentic and not be 'over-produced'.

So the key thing for me is the business of:

- asking questions appropriate to the people involved and to the situation at hand, using altruistic, compassionate, and empathic approaches, in order to get closer to what we wish to see in terms of more human behaviour in the workplace;

- working out how we can bring the ACE approach (Altruism, Compassion, and Empathy) to bear on the significant human challenges caused by the great disruptions of the day; *and*

- developing stories that can bring ACE principles to life in an accessible and engaging way so that people can learn and take inspiration from them.

PRACTICING THE ACE APPROACH – WHAT LEADERS CAN DO

Protecting and Preserving Purpose as Core to Organisational Culture and Success

We are living in a world disrupted by seismic changes wrought by waves of pandemics, accelerating climate change, and ongoing inequalities of many different kinds. Against this backdrop we also have a rapidly developing digital transformation which is bringing unimaginably positive change as well as many unintended and unforeseen consequences. In business, the era of shareholder value maximisation has more or less come to an end, with forward-looking corporations realising that the future needs to be different. Purpose – and the idea of purpose-led organisations – is resurgent after a previous blossoming 12 years or so ago in the aftermath of the Global Financial Crisis. This is to be welcomed. At the same time, it's important for us to notice that the presence of Purpose centre stage in corporate strategising *might be* the start of a pattern along the lines of what happened in the aftermath of the Global Financial Crisis. At that time, people heralded the opportunity to do things differently and for a while it seemed that might happen. But for the most part companies didn't change or mend their ways. If the pattern repeats itself, we might expect purpose to start to wane in intensity in five years' time or sooner. To prevent that from happening, we need to advocate now for a different kind of leadership to ensure that purpose stays core and that workplaces become more human. The CEO of Unilever, Alan Jope, has made it known on social media that he is convinced that the companies that will grow and thrive are the ones that put purpose centre-stage in all that they do. Unilever's purpose is to 'make sustainable living commonplace':

> We want to help create a world where everyone can live well within the natural limits of the planet. We're putting sustainable living at the heart of everything we do. That includes our brands and products, our standards of behaviour within and beyond Unilever, and our partnerships and advocacy efforts – which are driving transformational change across our value chain, and beyond. Brands must put 'purpose' over profit, new Unilever boss tells Davos.
>
> (Ben Marlowe, The Daily Telegraph, 22 January 2019)

I believe we can all benefit from a fresh approach, in which we recognise that old behaviours are unlikely to achieve what we need to achieve as we move into a potentially very different type of existence, one characterised by more frequent and quite possibly more destructive disruptions. Putting purpose first and underpinning it with values based on altruism, compassion, and empathy – is the way to go. This is the reason why ACE leadership skills have the potential to play a key role in changing workplace cultures – and society in general – for the better. In the next sections, we will look at what we can do in a practical sense to strengthen and develop these important attributes in service of more human workplaces – and the preservation of purpose as a key driver for organisations.

We will then take a look at three case studies from around the world to see how ACE qualities work in real workplace settings.

PRACTICAL ACTIVITIES TO PROMOTE ALTRUISM: SOME POINTERS

Get Started

- Start experimenting with simple actions.
- Be considerate of people when you're out and about. Vacate your seat on the bus for someone who needs it more.
- Get involved with community initiatives if you think that's something you would enjoy doing.
- Actively consider being less judgemental about people's actions and what they say on social media.
- Don't take things too seriously and try to cut people some slack when they say things you think are unwise.
- Try to cultivate a glass-half-full attitude to life.
- Get your news from a variety of sources and develop your capacity for active listening.
- The urgency around sustainability requires us to be altruistic: it means adopting the SDGs as a guiding set of principles. If you're a senior business leader, find out more about the SDGs and get a company audit done to figure out where you need to focus your efforts.
- Consider finding a compassion and altruism training programme. A 2013 study conducted by Helen Y. Weng et al. (2013, p. 1179) states:

   Our findings support the possibility that compassion and altruism can be viewed as trainable skills rather than stable traits.

PRACTICAL ACTIVITIES TO PROMOTE COMPASSION: SOME POINTERS

Develop Your Compassion

- Think about the different elements of compassion and attend to each of them (1)–(6)

    1. Be alive to the suffering of others.

    2. Avoid being judgemental.

    3. Think about how you manage distress, that is, how you deal with the stress that others are under – and specifically, its effect on you.

    4. Work on your empathy (see empathy below).

    5. Think about how to take compassionate action while always being aware of whether or not the subject of your compassion actually wants to engage with you on it!

    6. Explore self-compassion.

- Consider attending mindfulness classes.

- Consider becoming a mentor to someone.

- Consider joining a mental health charity – maybe even one that specialises in supporting mental health for a certain demographic.

- Be forgiving of yourself and the things you aren't proud of.

- Consider attending a self-compassion workshop.

PRACTICAL ACTIVITIES TO PROMOTE EMPATHY: SOME POINTERS

Enhance Your Capacity for Empathy

- Read as widely as you can about other people and their lives.

- Prioritise your curiosity about people.

- Watch films about other people and other places.

- Consider learning another language: it's a great way to connect with people different to you.

- Get involved with a virtual or in-person association, group, or club – this could include volunteering or simply involve spending times on a hobby, pastime, or with a sports-oriented community of people.

- Think about your interactions with your family, friends, work colleagues, clients, and others in your 'strong' and 'weak' tie networks. What's the scope for deepening relationships?

- Consider how you converse with people. Make an effort to ask them about their lives and use humility when it comes to talking about yours.

- Think about whether you could make a contribution as a coach or mentor to someone.

THREE MINI-CASE STUDIES TO ILLUSTRATE ACE IN ACTION IN ORGANISATIONS

Mini-Case Study Asia (1)   Singapore Airlines. *https://www.singaporeair. com/saar5/pdf/Investor-Relations/Annual-Report/sustainabilityreport1920. pdf*

Singapore Airlines (SIA) is the national flag-carrier of the Republic of Singapore and is one of the best airlines in the world. Like other players in the global airline industry, SIA has found itself facing huge disruption. Unlike other national airlines, and given that Singapore is a city-state, SIA does not have the benefit of an internal domestic air network to provide any compensation in the event that countries close their borders to incoming international flights. During 2020, larger countries with national airlines were still able to fly within their own domestic airspace. In July 2020, SIA posted its biggest ever loss (S$1.2 billion) in the first quarter (US$875m).

SIA was awarded the Most Attractive Employer in Singapore in 2019 by Randstad, a global leader in the HR services industry. There are 28,160 employees in the SIA Group in total and the organisation spends in the order of S$43.5 million in learning and development for its people per year. In 2018, the group made a Climate Action Pledge to declare its readiness to fight climate change together with other like-minded organisations and in addition, it launched an inaugural Environment Roadshow, in line with the Singapore government's designation of 2018 as the Year of Climate Action. In 2019, SIA established a Sustainability Office to enhance its sustainability strategy and framework and to encourage sustainability initiatives across the SIA Group. SIA aims to improve its operations from a sustainability standpoint across the whole value chain and to include the ecosystem within which SIA sits. The airline supports the United Nations 17 SDGs (the Sustainable Development Goals mentioned in *Expert Humans*, Chapter 2) and concentrates on SDGs 8, 12, and 13 (*Promote sustained, inclusive and sustainable economic growth, full and productive employment and decent work for all; Ensure sustainable consumption and production patterns,* and *Take urgent action to combat climate change and its impacts*).

The group has also set up KrisLab, which aims to position SIA as the world's leading digital airline. KrisLab works in partnership with small-, medium-, and large companies to develop digital solutions for the world of aviation.

In addition to supporting the sustainability agenda (thereby role-modelling altruism in a corporate setting), the airline demonstrates its commitment to its staff through an excellent training and development system, although with the group experiencing huge cost pressures as a result of the pandemic, cost-cutting initiatives have had to be brought in across the business. SIA won praise for its agile actions over the redeployment of cabin staff in the battle against COVID-19 (thereby demonstrating compassion): these staff provided support at key Singapore hospitals in a variety of roles for which of course they were eminently suited (highly customer-facing and people-centric).

I have been able to experience SIA as a customer and also a visitor (to their learning and development hub). While walking the corridors in the hub, I was struck by the friendliness of the place and the practice of the SIA staff cheerily greeting visitors with a 'good morning!' as they walked past. Some might say cynically that these acts of friendliness are taught behaviours – and maybe they are. But the experience is still impressive, and the memory of the warm welcome remains. SIA is a highly efficient corporate entity and as such I think it is a good example of an organisation striving to do well on sustainability and learning and development – two things which will help in the fight on climate change and also on developing new leadership skills for the future.

Mini-Case Study Europe (2)   WildHearts Group, Glasgow, Scotland.
https://www.wildheartsgroup.com/our-impact/

WildHearts Group, with its headquarters in Glasgow, consists of a portfolio of companies providing a range of office products to organisations across the United Kingdom. The big thing about WildHearts is that the profits from their customers' spend goes to fund the activities of the WildHearts Foundation, which is a registered charity. The Foundation carries out a range of social initiatives and projects which include giving young people in the UK key development and employability skills – through to tackling gender inequality in the developing world. In Chapter 2 of *Expert Humans*, we looked at the issue of gender inequality as one of the key disruptors in our world today – a persistent challenge which WildHearts is addressing with a real sense of urgency. The WildHearts' 'Start-Her' Strategy supports women and girls in countries like Malawi via three key initiatives: Enterprise, Education, and Health. Women are given access to financial and enterprise training; children are given essential tools for learning; and the health programme provides girls with essential menstrual health products and education – as the WildHearts people say, emphatically,: [To ensure that once the girls are in school] '... they stay there'.

Sustainability is a major part of the activities of WildHearts which tackles more than 50% of the United Nations SDGs. The group holds the strong conviction that 'business can and should be a force for good.... We believe in the creativity and resilience of humanity'.

WildHearts' SDGs

WildHearts is a great example of a company working with ACE attributes while it addresses the following 10 SGDs: *No poverty; Zero hunger; Good health and wellbeing; Quality education; Gender equality; Decent work and economic growth; Reduced inequalities; Sustainable cities and communities;* and *Climate action and Partnerships for the Goals.* The aspect of the company that really excited me was the outlining of what Dr Mick Jackson, the CEO calls: 'Compassionate Disruption', in an article to explain how he sees this as a major trend in our world today. Mick says:

Consider the following stats and their effect on the fundamentals of business success – attracting customers, motivating staff and attracting talent:

Attracting and Retaining Customers

84% of consumers believe that companies should do more for society – Ipsos Mori

A company's revenue can increase by 20% as a result of their Corporate Responsibility Strategy – Babson Social Innovation Lab & IO Sustainability

Engaging your Team

86% of workers believe it is important that their employer is responsible to society – Ipsos Mori

Staff turnover can be reduced by 50% by implementing Corporate Responsibility effectively – Babson Social Innovation Lab & IO Sustainability

Attracting Future Talent

75% of the global workforce by 2025 will want to work for organisations that make a positive contribution to society – Deloitte Millennial Survey

75% of millennials say they would take a pay cut to work for a more responsible company – Cone Millennial Cause Group

Not Business as Usual

These stats strongly suggest that our attitudes towards business and the role it should play in the world have fundamentally changed. Our behaviours are changing accordingly. They are driving our decisions as to what companies we want to buy from and what companies we want to work for.

This should be a wake-up call for any credible business leader. As I say to my peers, 'If you are not compelling customers to buy from you, inspiring your current team to deliver their best for you and attracting the best talent to join and stay with you, then you need to go.' Ultimately that is your job.

'This should be a wake-up call for any credible business leader'. Mick puts it as forcefully as Rudi Plettinx did in Chapter 2. Altruism, compassion, and empathy are the critical leadership skills we need in this disrupted world.

Mini-Case Study: North America (3)   Workday

Workday is headquartered in Pleasanton, California, and was established about 15 years ago. It has come a long way. In 2020, it achieved #5 place in Fortune's *100 Best Companies to Work For*; in 2019 it was #3 in Great Place to Work's *Europe's Best Workplaces* and in 2020 it was #1 on the Fortune Future 50 list of companies best positioned for long-term growth. The CEO Aneel Bhusri explains:

> *Workday was founded on a disruptive idea: to put people at the center of enterprise software ... coupled with a relentless pursuit of innovation ... in light of today's global challenges, innovation plays a key role in doing our part to help solve some of the world's toughest problems. Aneel Bhusri, Letter from the CEO, Workday website:* https://www.workday.com/en-us/company/about-workday/our-story-leadership.html

Workday is active in all of the areas that we have looked at during the course of this book: it is at the heart of digital transformation (in enterprise software – financial and human resources); it puts people at the centre of its business (a human workplace recognised by a number of respected external bodies); and it operates (like WildHearts) a Foundation, the Workday Foundation.

The Foundation's work attends to four of the SDGs: *No Poverty*; *Quality Education*; *Decent Work and Economic Growth*; and *Sustainable Cities and Communities*.

As a values-driven company, Workday's Core Values guide leadership decisions, as well as day-to-day interactions. Every year anywhere from 500 to 800 new Workday managers come together globally to learn about Workday's values directly from the Founders and the Executive Team. Workday's first and most important value is 'Employees' in that happy employees lead to happy customers and more thriving communities. Another value which contributes to the development of a human workplace is 'Fun' – 'a core value that's ingrained into the way we work'. Under the rubric 'Fun' the company includes 'Creating Connections', 'Clubs', and 'Family' – which cover Friday get-togethers by the staff, over 100 Clubs of different kinds and even a Bring Your Dog to Workday Day (the dogs are known as 'Workdogs').

As Chris Ernst, Vice-President of Leadership & Organizational Effectiveness puts it,

> *What Workday is proving is that when you operate business with principles of altruism, compassion, and empathy, you grow and win even within the highly competitive sector of 21st century enterprise technology.*

This looks like a human workplace in action and should be seen as a role model for other organisations.

CRITICAL LEADERSHIP SKILLS FOR A DISRUPTED WORLD

Table 12 offers a summary of where ACE skills can have the most impact. While altruism, compassion, and empathy are all needed to address a range of global disruptions, there might be value in providing some focus in order to sharpen our efforts.

SUSTAINABILITY OF THE PLANET AND ALTRUISM

There are some great initiatives being taken by committed and forward-looking individuals and organisations in respect of sustainability and all the related issues which sit underneath it such as global warming, energy, water security, and many others (as captured and codified in the United Nations SDGs, to which I have referred frequently in *Expert Humans*). We know that companies and businesses appreciate the need to run their operations in a sustainable manner for a myriad of good reasons, and not least because it makes

Table 12: Critical Leadership Skills for a Disrupted World – Impact of ACE.

Disruption	Sustainability of the Planet	Global Human Health	Inequality	Digital Transformation	Erosion of Trust
Critical Leadership Skills					
Altruism	■				■
Compassion		■		■	
Empathy			■		

good business sense, given the related impact it has on employer branding and the effect that has in turn on the perception of customers and employees about the organisation in question. But above and beyond all of this, the thing that we can use as a beacon or anchor point for all of our efforts in sustainability has got to be altruism. We can marshal all of our arguments and put forth scientific data in support of all of those arguments, which is great and just as it should be – but what really should make the difference is that we are doing what we are doing out of an altruistic sense of duty and responsibility towards all those human beings who will come after us.

GLOBAL HUMAN HEALTH AND COMPASSION

We are living at a time when the danger represented by global health concerns, including but not limited to pandemics (I am thinking of food and water security and how the lack of these can adversely impact communities and damage human health) – is at an all-time high. The scale of human suffering and grief is monumental and defies full comprehension by ordinary human beings. We watch the news, we follow breaking stories on our digital devices and we wonder how best we can respond, in an effort to make a difference. I think the aspect of 'making a difference' can quite justifiably come in many shapes and sizes and at many different levels of society. If you happen to be the prime minister of a country you have the power to change things for the better, and to help the citizens of your country in a very direct way. But you don't have to be the prime minister of a country to be able to make a difference, of course. I mentioned earlier in *Expert Humans* that it is important for us to be making a positive difference in the little corner of the cosmos that we occupy: if we can do more, well then so much the better. The ACE quality that wraps around all these things, for me, is the quality and attribute of compassion. No matter how senior or junior you are, no matter whether you are rich or poor, compassion is the thing that we will need the most of in the years to come. Within this, we must include self-compassion too and the good things that it can bring us if we practice it.

INEQUALITY AND EMPATHY

I have spoken earlier in *Expert Humans* about how I see ongoing lack of equality – in all its manifestations – as one of the most pernicious disruptors in our world. The lack of opportunity for women around the world, the conditions under which women have to eke out an existence and the vicious nature of patriarchies, still extant in our world – is something we must continue to rail at and to try our best to change, even if what we are able to achieve is small and modest. We must stand up for racial equality and the rights of all communities – and look to bring into our organisations all the wonderfully talented people who happen to see the world in a different way to the majority of us. The ACE quality we can deploy – the one that we can strengthen and turn into a powerful tool for change – is empathy. We need to work harder to try to see what we can't see, and to try to put ourselves in the position of others.

DIGITAL TRANSFORMATION, COMPASSION, AND EMPATHY

Our world continues to progress at breakneck speed when it comes to digital transformation. Prior to the global health pandemics, it was digital disruption that preoccupied many of us and in fact it still does – the global health challenges we have experienced have, if anything, accelerated our march towards a supremely digital future. Many observers have noted that certain digital changes that were on the cards but that were thought of as needing at least a few years to put in place – are now happening. Digital doctor appointments are commonplace; workshops, events, conferences, and events – all of these things happen via digital platforms of various kinds.

Some people heralded the implementation of Work From Home as a watershed moment that would change the world of work forever. At the same time, others would point out that 'going to work' isn't just about the work: it's also about patterns and habits, leaving a trail in the world as you make your way to and fro – and perhaps most importantly, it's about having human contact. This is why I think the ACE qualities we are going to need to draw on are compassion and empathy. There will be many unforeseen consequences of digital advancement and while I personally am all for it, I think it is worth recognising that for some people, it will bring different, and not entirely welcome, things. We will hear more about a felt loss of empathy by workers whose jobs have been supplanted by chatbots; and we will hear more stories about loneliness and societal fragmentation where networks get constricted and our sphere of human friendships starts to diminish (for both strong and weak tie networks). Social media will mitigate and replace, but not completely. Hence there will be a growing need for more compassion and empathy.

EROSION OF TRUST – ALTRUISM, COMPASSION, AND EMPATHY

In Chapter 1 of Expert Humans, I concluded by saying:

> *Trust is in short supply in our world today. And I believe that the development of truly 'Expert Human' skills has got to be one of the biggest enablers of trust-building.*

I strongly believe this to be so. Without trust, everything falls apart. For this reason, I think we are going to need to deploy all three ACE attributes in our quest to create more trust in society and in our workplaces. Trust has been battered over the past decade through accelerated geopolitical turmoil; domestic political upheaval; continued corporate wrongdoing; unbridled, selfish attitudes, and behaviour in the workplace, featuring fearsome and brutal managers and leaders; and vicious activity on social media and cyber-space in general. Applying altruism, compassion, and empathy won't solve everything, but the world will be better for it.

In the concluding chapter of *Expert Humans*, we will look at what might be coming our way in the next 5–10 years – and how we might expect a more human way of being and working might evolve.

10

WHERE DO WE GO FROM HERE?

- What we can expect in the next 5–10 years and what we can do to mitigate the disruption to come.
- Final thoughts and reflections.

DISRUPTION TO COME

Donald Rumsfeld famously talked about the existence of 'known–knowns' and 'unknown–unknowns' at a US Department of Defense news briefing on 12 February 2002 regarding the lack of evidence linking the government of Iraq with the supply of weapons of mass destruction to terrorist organisations – borrowing on the thinking behind Johari Window which I mentioned in Chapter 4. In this concluding chapter, we will look at some of the 'known knowns' around the great disruptors of our time and do our best to consider what some of the 'unknown unknowns' might be.

'Unknown unknowns' can also be termed 'Black Swan events'. More about that later.

SUSTAINABILITY OF THE PLANET

The UN's Sustainable Development Goals (SDGs) provide a useful summary of the key global challenges facing the human race today. At a practical level, as we have seen in the three mini-case studies in Chapter 9, the

SDGs can provide organisations with the foundational elements of their own sustainability plan. We should urge all organisations to look at their business models, their supply chains and their current impact on the world by using the SDGs as a means to zero in on what their contribution to improving the situation could be. Organisations need to start somewhere and to have a logical base that employees and other stakeholders can buy into and understand. It's clear that a single organisation cannot attend to every issue, but with focus and commitment, we can look to an 'agglomeration effect' of each small change contributing to positive transformation on a much bigger scale. So what is the prognosis for the world in the next 5–10 years and what could the ACE approach offer? The challenge is clear. On its website, NASA quotes the following, for the avoidance of doubt:

> *Scientific evidence for warming of the climate system is unequivocal.*
> Intergovernmental Panel on Climate Change

NASA goes on to say:

> *The current warming trend is of particular significance because most of it is extremely likely (greater than 95 percent probability) to be the result of human activity since the mid-20th century and proceeding at a rate that is unprecedented over decades to millennia.*
> IPCC Fifth Assessment Report, Summary for Policymakers

We know that the heat-trapping nature of carbon dioxide and other gases affects the transfer of infrared energy through the atmosphere: as a result of this, there is no question that increased levels of greenhouse gases cause the Earth to warm.

And we know we have a huge problem on our hands. The good news is that we have some assets that I think will play a major part in mitigating the sustainability challenges we face. These assets include large, medium, and small companies that are all determined to play their part in the greatest battle of our times.

An example of one of these assets is the multinational company Acciona, headquartered in Madrid which, as a sustainable infrastructure developer, is at the forefront of sustainability. The business of the company broadly covers construction, concessions, water and services, with a big focus on renewable energy. The company follows the SDGs and from 2019 decided to focus on SDGs 6, 7, 9, 11, and 13 which are, respectively: *Clean water and sanitation*; *Affordable and clean energy*; *Industry, Innovation and infrastructure*; *Cities and sustainable communities*; and *Climate action*. It is good to see such a major company leading the way in this fashion and also to note, in its Human Resources and Occupational Health and Safety Policy, that there is a focus on the following, among many positive elements, in what constitutes a human place to work:

- Equality, diversity and inclusion – bringing in people who are 'at risk of social inclusion' and people with disabilities

- The hiring of local workers – to bring value to the societies where the company is active

- A strong focus on health and safety in the workplace given the nature of the company's business and

- Personal health and wellbeing of all staff.

From: Acciona, *https://www.acciona.com/about-acciona/about-us/*

Companies like Acciona set a high bar for others to emulate and follow. Their actions reflect the spirit of altruism, compassion and empathy.

Another organisation which I have referenced previously in *Expert Humans* is the WBCSD (the World Business Council for Sustainable Development). The WBCSD has launched a key initiative which I believe will be crucial for the future, namely the promotion of the circular economy:

> *The future of business is circular and there's no room for waste in it … our goal is to build a critical mass of engagement within and across business to move the circular economy to deliver and scale solutions need to build a sustainable world.*
>
> *From: WBCSD website:* https://www.wbcsd.org/Programs/
> Circular-Economy

The idea is that by 2050, as detailed in the WBCSD's Vision 2050, created in 2010, 'not a particle of waste should exist'. The aim of the initiative is to advocate for a set of 'must-haves' – the things that must happen over the coming decade to make a sustainable planetary society possible. These include:

[...]incorporating the costs of externalities, starting with carbon, ecosystem services and water, into the structure of the marketplace; doubling agricultural output without increasing the amount of land or water used; halting deforestation and increasing yields from planted forests: halving carbon emissions worldwide (based on 2005 levels) by 2050 through a shift to low-carbon energy systems and improved demand-side energy efficiency, and providing universal access to low-carbon mobility.

WBCSD: *Vision 2050 at* https://www.wbcsd.
org/Overview/About-us/Vision2050/Resources/
Vision-2050-The-new-agenda-for-business

The task in hand is clear. We just need to get on with it. The WBCSD underscores what is needed by citing an article from Forbes by William Sisson, Executive Director WBCSD North America, which first appeared on 24 April 2020:

In this [pandemic] crisis, it is crucial to support and show compassion toward each other. It is equally essential to continue working on sustainable development.

Compassion is clearly a key requirement of our disrupted times. At the same time, for sustainability into the future, we are also going to have to have people and corporations acting altruistically. Our actions now might not have any 'payback' for us *right now*, but they will as far as future generations are concerned.

GLOBAL HUMAN HEALTH

The global human health crisis brought on by the COVID-19 pandemic has caused tremendous hardship for many around the world. Very few countries have been spared. If we can try to salvage something good from all of this, it would be to recall all the truly human things we have witnessed: the clapping for health workers around the world; singing opera for the pleasure of your neighbours in Italy; people sewing masks around the clock in places where masks are not so readily available; the global concert of music superstars organised by Lady Gaga: the list goes on.

At the same time it is sobering to consider the view of *The Black Swan* author and thinker Nassim Nicholas Taleb who pointed out that the pandemic of 2019/2020 was not an event that was unpredictable: it was entirely predictable because the world had seen such events before (like SARS). Which means that pandemics can and will happen again.

The key thing is to be prepared and to exercise compassion and empathy for those directly and indirectly affected by these quickly moving and fast-developing viruses.

One of the biggest killers in history, smallpox, was eventually tamed and eradicated through the discovery of a vaccine. Malaria, thought to have killed about half the number of humans who have ever lived, is getting to the point where a pathway to eradicate it has become a distinct possibility. That said, here is an excerpt of a discussion hosted on 23 August 2019 by Christian Lindmeier, Communications Officer for the World Health Organisation and conducted with a panel of experts who explain to listeners just how difficult the process of eradication is. (It is interesting to note that this discussion took place only a few months before the COVID-19 pandemic broke out in Wuhan). In the discussion, Pedro Alonso, the director of the WHO's global malaria programme, answers a question about the key challenges of malaria eradication:

> So the first response to your question is, we're dealing with a biologically very complex organism that mutates, that evades the immune response, that is transmitted by a mosquito and for which several of the biological clues we still don't quite well understand, simply because of its complexity. So I would say that's number one; we're dealing with a really complex enemy.
>
> The second one is, this enemy takes place often in the hardest-to-reach areas, affecting impoverished communities with little access to health systems and therefore the second big issue is contextually this is the place where you don't want to have this type of fight; where it's hard to reach, poorer communities, impoverished with lack of health systems.
>
> The third one is because we don't have good tools, we don't have the type of vaccines that other diseases have, highly efficacious and very safe. We have very imperfect tools. So all of this put together means we're fighting what some have termed the biggest enemy of mankind in history – some have even dared to say that half of mankind that has died up to now has died of malaria so we're talking of a big one, a

very complex one that takes place in a very complex environment and
for which we don't really have tools.
From: World Health Organisation: Discussion on
Malaria Eradication, 23 August 2019, transcript

If our challenges with malaria are anything to go by, the battle with COVID-19 is likely to be a long and protracted one. Unlike malaria, however, COVID-19 travels and destroys economies and human activity in a way that malaria has not done – although malaria has exerted its malignant influence in terms of obstructing economic development and hampering progress of the countries in which it is most widespread. COVID-19 will cast a long shadow for a very long time to come.

In this sense, it makes it even more important that we behave altruistically when effective vaccines come into play. And all the while we need to continue to exhibit compassion and empathy to those who suffer loss – of loved ones, jobs, and security.

There is also a growing sense among many in the global health arena – among them people who work in humanitarian organisations – who worry that the compassion that brought them into the field is getting buried under a welter of other pressures, leading to burnout – physical and mental exhaustion. Humanitarians working in health and in disaster zones have shared that they wonder what ever happened to compassion. It seems that for them the immediate challenge is to rediscover compassion and practice it among their own team first. Doing so will benefit the people – the dispossessed, the refugees, the sick and injured – those who the team is ultimately there to serve. It's the 'put your own oxygen mask on first before helping others' approach.

INEQUALITY

I have used the term 'inequality' to embrace the challenges of all groups who, given the nature of the societies in which they live and the often-unique challenges they face, are disadvantaged, treated inequitably and often persecuted simply for being who they are. Everyone has a right to be able to 'find their place' such that they feel loved, 'at home' and able to fulfil their potential. I would like to believe that everyone would agree that this is a highly desirable outcome, but the fact remains of course that there are forces – individuals, groups, and organisations – who don't see things this way and who actively try to disadvantage, control or even destroy those who do not conform to their way of seeing the world. In extreme cases, such orientations are manifested in hate crimes and violence while in other cases, people who see the world differently or experience the world differently are marginalised, discriminated against and denied their basic human rights. The assault on equality has been turbocharged by social media and fuelled by populist politicians who sow discord and distrust. These are things that we hear about every day. For many who suffer unfair or inhumane treatment, it is relentless. It happens every day. What a huge mountain for us as humans to even try to scale. Fortunately, the world is also populated by amazing individuals and organisations whose efforts are helping to chip away at the edifice.

One person I have been lucky enough to meet and spend time with is Marina Cantacuzino, the founder of a UK-based secular charity called The Forgiveness Project whose Founding Patrons are the late Dame Anita Roddick and Archbishop Desmond Tutu. The Forgiveness Project 'collects and shares stories from both victims/survivors and perpetrators of crime and conflict who have rebuilt their lives following hurt and trauma' (https://www.theforgivenessproject.com/our-purpose/). Through collecting testimonies that bear witness to the resilience of the human spirit, which act as a powerful antidote to narratives of hate and dehumanisation, The Forgiveness Project helps to present alternatives to cycles of conflict, violence, crime and injustice.

This is an incredible purpose.

The Forgiveness Project explains its Purpose further:

> At the heart of The Forgiveness Project is an understanding that restorative narratives have the power to transform lives; not only supporting people to deal with issues in their own lives, but also building a climate of tolerance, resilience, hope and empathy. The Forgiveness Project at https://www.theforgivenessproject.com/our-purpose/

Empathy: This is what is needed. And where better demonstrated than by one of The Forgiveness Project's core activities, the RESTORE programme:

> RESTORE is The Forgiveness Project's award-winning, intensive group-based intervention programme that supports prisoners in their process of change towards desistance from crime. RESTORE achieves this through a highly skilled facilitation team that includes both victims and perpetrators of crime.

- The Forgiveness Project has nine years of experience in delivering RESTORE within the Criminal Justice System, reaching 3,300 participants inclusive of 185 prison officers.

  For most prisoners, time inside is simply an experience to be endured. So there is something extraordinary about a course, which sets out to ask prisoners to examine the most profound and difficult issues imaginable. In my view, RESTORE can start a process of personal reflection without which rehabilitation and restoration are impossible. – Peter Dawson, Governor, HMP High Down (2007–2013)

This is an example of how even the most seemingly intractable, hopeless situations can be turned around – as long as there is empathy, and action in the form of compassion. I am pleased to have been able to help support this kind of prisoner rehabilitation work, if only in small part.

DIGITAL TRANSFORMATION

In Chapter 1, I speculated about the possibility of an AI winter, meaning us heading into a period where the pace of advancement in AI is potentially going to slow down, and I asked whether this might be an ideal time to play catch-up in terms of human skills development in organisations. In an AI winter, big tech advances slow, the interest shown by the general public starts to wane, excitement levels dissipate and crucially, zest for investment starts to lose its fizz.

Well, I am not sure we will enter an AI winter but perhaps an AI autumn is more likely; this is where the tendency to lump all digital innovations into one big AI starts to be replaced by a more measured attitude to AI and what it can do – think less showy robots and more in-the-background AI, where AI merges into processes and systems in a less perceptible way. The pandemic of 2020 had an accelerating effect on certain aspects of the digital transformation such that for the majority of people, the use of platforms like Zoom, Microsoft Teams, and Google Meet – have become second nature, nothing special. The catch-up in terms of human skills development, which I referenced in Chapter 1, is now happening: there is more questioning than ever about the merits and demerits of in-person meetings and virtual ones; we have been through the stage of virtual being said to be 'more or less just like in-person' to a more questioning stage where considerations about 'how people show up' and 'eye-contact' and 'overall body language', not to mention a new protocol around 'Zoom etiquette' – are coming to the fore. The excitement and novelty of 'Work From Home' has faded for many people as the realisation beds down that work – for a lot of people – is not just about work, but about human contact and interaction. If not for the unpredictable nature of the pandemic with its sudden resurgences, I think many more people would sooner re-establish their working patterns and routines while those people who were working from home before the pandemic will more or less continue according to their previous practice. What continues to be a concern is the increase in mental ill-health in the workplace year on year, which was already a concern in pre-pandemic days. For some people, lockdowns and isolation have exacerbated an existing mental fragility. It is a time for empathy, compassion and understanding.

A July 2020 report by the CIPD had this to say about lockdown life:

> *It can be hard to pick up on body language and expressions in virtual meetings, which can hamper creativity. This also presents a challenge for managers to communicate meaningfully and for leaders to be visible:*

> *'As a line manager I really struggle to empathise sometimes and need the visual body language clues to moderate my tone and style.'*
> *Manager, 40+*

> *Managers must be mindful of not forgetting about quieter members of the team who may not always be comfortable asking for help. These findings indicate a role for people professionals in providing employees and managers with guidance to support effective use of virtual communication and collaboration. Team cohesion is also being threatened by lack of face-to-face interactions. Many employees miss casual water cooler conversations that often spark creative solutions to problems and opportunities to use colleagues as a sounding board:*

> *'I am really missing seeing other people and the social interaction.'*
> *Worker, 18–39*

> *Most focus group respondents felt that they are working longer hours due to a lack of delineation between work and home life, which is particularly a problem for those working with international clients:*

'I think as we are working from home, senior management expect you to be online all day every day, including weekends.' Manager, 40+

In terms of other aspects of wellbeing, spending extended time at a desk with inappropriate seating is causing physical problems, including strained eyes and bad posture. Managers are also worried about people not taking their annual leave. However, some employees said that they are eating better, saving money and feel physically better as a result of lower pollution. From Workplace Technology – The Employee Experience, CIPD, July 2020

As for AI in the workplace over the next five years: I think there will be an acceleration in tech practices that I think people will accept and fold into their normal working practices, with some possible hiccups along the way. In typical organisations, one area which is ripe for disruption is the HR function. This is in many ways the part of the organisation where people and technology come together (or some might say, it is where they collide). The IBM Smarter Workforce Institute, in a report entitled *The Business Case for AI in HR*, listed how AI is being used:

- To solve pressing business challenges

- To attract and develop new skills

- To improve the employee experience

- To provide strong decision support

- To use HR budgets as efficiently as possible.

IBM Smarter Workforce Institute: The Business Case for AI in HR, November 2018

In practical terms, AI can be used to improve the quality of the recruitment and screening process, with chatbots guiding applicants through the early stages and keeping them updated along the way. The savings in human contact time to respond to applicant enquiries and field calls from people wondering how things are going – are substantial. Candidates for jobs report enjoying aspects of the automated recruitment process and they like the way they can check their progress 24/7 by talking with the chatbot whenever they want. There are AI applications available to assist in aligning compensation packages more accurately to business strategy and objectives, which in turn can increase the level of transparency and contribute positively to the employee experience overall. AI can also help employees to navigate their own career planning within large companies thanks to greater clarity on possible career transitions, including ones that might not be so obvious.

Some companies have experienced issues with the introduction of AI into the recruitment process whereby the algorithm has been found to be biased, as in the case of one company which suddenly found it was not shortlisting any female candidates: it was discovered after investigation that the algorithm was actively screening out women due to a misconfiguration.

THE FUTURE OF WORK

Reports such as The World Economic Forum's (WEF) *Future of Work 2018* provide us with a snapshot of what we can expect in the next 2–5 years as a result of the impact of AI on the workforce.

The WEF concurs with the idea that AI will ultimately create more jobs than it will destroy. In 2022, the top emerging jobs are envisaged to be:

Top emerging jobs:

1. Data analysts and Scientists.

2. AI and Machine Learning Specialists.

3. General and Operations Managers.

4. Software and Applications Developers and Analysts.

5. Sales and Marketing Professionals.

6. Big Data Specialists.

7. Digital Transformation Specialists.

8. New Technology Specialists.

9. Organisational Developments Specialists.

10. Information Technology Services.

The jobs that will decline are estimated to be:

Declining jobs:

1. Data Entry Clerks.

2. Accounting, Bookkeeping, and Payroll Clerks.

3. Administrative and Executive Secretaries.

4. Assembly and Factory Workers.

5. Client Information and Customer Service Workers.

6. Business Services and Administration Managers.

7. Accountants and Auditors.

8. Material-Recording and Stock-keeping Clerks.

9. General and Operations Managers.

10. Postal Service Clerks.

WEF estimates the number of emerging jobs to be around 133 million while the number of declining jobs is estimated at around 75 million (Future of Work 2018, World Economic Forum). Other observers have provided different estimates but the consensus is that more jobs will be created than will be lost. In terms of skills that will be needed, WEF's Future of Work 2018 paints the following picture:

Growing skills include:

1. Analytical thinking.

2. Active learning and learning strategies.

3. Creativity, originality, and initiative.

4. Technology design and programming.

5. Critical thinking and analysis.

6. Complex problem-solving.

7. Leadership and social influence.

8. Emotional intelligence.

9. Reasoning, problem-solving, and ideation.

10. Systems analysis and evaluation.

While declining skills include:

1. Manual dexterity, endurance, and precision.

2. Memory, verbal, auditory, and spatial abilities.

3. Management of financial, material resources.

4. Technology installation and maintenance.

5. Reading, writing, math, and active listening.

6. Management of personnel.

7. Quality control and safety awareness.

8. Coordination and time management.

9. Visual, auditory, and speech abilities.

10. Technology use, monitoring, and control.

It is interesting to note that *Emotional intelligence* is called out as a specific skill (in at number 8). This is an encouraging trend and underscores the ascendancy of ACE skills in the future workplace. It is also good to see Leadership and social influence at number 7 too.

EROSION OF TRUST

I have included 'erosion of trust' as one of the big disruptors of our time because it is happening at many levels in human society today, starting with political erosion of trust at the top, compounded by an erosion of trust in governments, corporations and other organisations, and further exacerbated by the crisis of trust felt by individuals in the workplace and about different systems, sectors, and parts of society: sports, entertainment, and education are three examples from recent years.

TRUST IN POLITICS

People have always been cynical about politicians. Back in 1990s Japan, I recall a taxi ride in Tokyo when the chatty driver decided to regale me with his take on Japanese politics at that time (I think most people would agree that taxi drivers in capital cities are never backwards in coming forwards in terms of sharing their views on any number of things – but politics especially!). He was bemoaning the fact that the ruling Liberal Democratic Party was – in his view – becoming nothing more than a vehicle for the political classes to line their pockets, treating the people of Japan like fools. In Japanese he told me – in a play on words – that Japanese politicians had become 'purveyors of politics', that is, they treated politics (with its favours, duties, and obligations) as a commodity, their backing, support and their word to be sold to the highest bidder. 'Seijika [politicians] wa seijiya [sellers of politics] ni narimashita'. Politicians have become Sellers of Politics. I think this is something with which people around the world can readily identify. In this kind of climate, trust simply evaporates, as we know. The other 'trust killer' is incompetence. If we believe our leaders to be incompetent and lacking in compassion and empathy, then trust simply dies. This is something happening in many countries around the world. The good news is that there are some good role models of exemplary compassionate leadership like Jacinda Ardern (as mentioned in Chapter 8).

TRUST IN THE WORKPLACE AND TRUST IN BUSINESSES

Inside the Organisation

A famous quotation from the great management thinker Peter Drucker put it like this:

> The leaders who work most effectively, it seems to me, never say 'I.' And that's not because they have trained themselves not to say 'I.' They don't think 'I.' They think 'we'; they think 'team.' They understand their job to be to make the team function. They accept responsibility and don't sidestep it, but 'we' gets the credit ... This is what creates trust, what enables you to get the task done.
>
> • Peter Drucker, author of *Managing for the Future from Habits for Wellbeing (2020) – 20 Inspirational Leadership Quotes*

We also know that creating psychological safety at work is an effective way to build up trust between team members and in the leaders of the organisation. It is also intrinsically linked to ethical leadership as we noted in Chapter 8. One thing builds on and reinforces the other. It also helps externally too.

Outside the Organisation

We have seen in different stories and mini-case studies in *Expert Humans* that ACE attributes really begin at home, that is, if the leadership of an organisation is recognised internally as practicing ACE behaviours, this will become manifest in the organisational persona – people outside the organisation will hear what goes on inside it and they will want to be associated with that organisation because of the good and solid reputation it has developed. A virtuous circle will form and what happens externally will reinforce what happens internally. People want to feel proud of the organisation they work in and spend a lot of time thinking about. Our task is to facilitate that.

IN THE YEARS TO COME

The World Economic Forum (Future of Work 2018) lists five things we will need to watch and be aware of in the years to come. These are:

1. That automation, robotisation and digitisation look different across different industries.

2. There is a net positive outlook for jobs – amid significant job disruption.

3. The division of labour between humans, machines and algorithms is shifting fast.

4. New tasks at work are driving demand for new skills.

5. We will all need to become lifelong learners.

(The Future of Work 2018, World Economic Forum).
The projected rate of automation is astonishing too.

Table 13: Rate of Automation: Division of Labour as Share of Hours Spent (%).

	Human	Machine
2018	71	29
2022	58	42
2025	48	52

The disruption – the shift – is clear. And the opportunity to leverage AI to open up space for us to develop our emotional intelligence – our humanity – is also clear.

A 2018 report from Accenture and The Aspen Institute emphasises this transformation, stating:

> Human skills are surging.
>
> *As companies rapidly adopt Artificial Intelligence (AI) and related technologies, some job roles will be done exclusively by humans while others will be taken on by intelligent automation. But most emerging roles will be fulfilled by people and machines working together in the dynamic space Accenture calls 'the missing middle'.*
>
> *These roles will require people to apply higher level human skills. Our analysis of how skills have evolved in the 12 years to 2016 shows that more than half of jobs in the U.S. need more high-level creativity, 47 percent require more complex reasoning and 36 percent need* more socio-emotional skills. *From: Advancing Missing Middle Skills for Human–AI collaboration, The Aspen Institute and Accenture 2018*

More socio-emotional skills: The signs are there that we are on the right track if we can encourage the adoption of ACE skills. The Accenture (2018) report also offers this observation from Rachael Rekert, Director of Machine Assistance, Autodesk:

> *The companies that do not associate AI with EI (emotional intelligence) are going to miss the mark.*

And an article by McKinsey Japan, *The Future of Work in Japan: Accelerating automation after COVID-19*, 1 July 2020 notes that 56% of activities and occupations in Japan are highly susceptible to automation (such as processing data, collecting data, predictable physical work as performed by payroll officers, legal support workers, mortgage originators, production workers and machine operators). The least susceptible roles are ones that involve managing others such as the CEO role or project manager role (only 6% susceptible). In a country like Japan, which has a shrinking workforce and an aging population, the opportunities afforded by the positive disruption of AI (digital disruption) coupled with global health disruption (the global pandemic) are game-changing:

> *[...]organisations will need to operate with flexibility – both in where people work and in when they do so. For Japanese companies, that will create new opportunities to recruit people who could not or would not work under less flexible conditions. Potential recruits include parents with small children, people in other countries, and those whose personal or professional priorities make it difficult to commit to a traditional office job. Digital innovation can further enhance flexibility by giving leaders new tools to foster culture, manage teams, and safeguard cybersecurity. From: McKinsey Japan, The Future of Work in Japan: Accelerating automation after COVID-19, 1 July 2020*

The authors of the McKinsey Japan article, Maya Horii and Yasuaki Sakurai, suggest that,

> *For Japan, recovering from the public-health crisis is both a challenge and an opportunity to accelerate the automation that is critical to the country's economic growth. If leaders in the public and private sectors can work together to prioritise action, Japan is likely not just to recover but also to lead the way in the next digital revolution.*

And not only more socio-emotional skills: The march of digital transformation and the fundamental shifts we are seeing in the world of work will require an even broader set of skills – a 'global mindset' – the ability to interact with people in mutually beneficial ways across borders created by time and space. In an article in People Matters (September 2020), Joyce Jenkins (2020) shares the following:

> *Resolving the current disruption and dealing with the looming economic and environmental crises will require the collaboration across borders of the world's best talent. Maximizing the potential of the complex and volatile global marketplace of the 21st Century will also require a range of international skills, perspectives and intercultural competence, along with a 'global mindset' to lead and facilitate effective work and communication.*

I have no doubt that the development of such global mindsets can be supported by encouraging more altruism, compassion and empathy.

TO CONCLUDE

In *Expert Humans: Critical Leadership Skills for a Disrupted World*, we have looked at five major areas ('Disruptors') where disruption is happening: we've considered the implications and started to think about how we might start to address the different sources of disruption, namely:

- *Sustainability* (disruption of the planet from an environmental perspective). This requires an urgent and disruptive response to make us do things differently – a supremely altruistic response because the good that we could do, will benefit generations to come.

- *Global Human Health* (disruption on a global scale of our way of life and our economic system). This needs a sea-change in attitudes (recognition of the narrowing of the human-wild animal divide, erosion of animal habitats) if we are to mitigate the potential for future pandemics: the situation requires compassion and empathy now, and altruism for the future.

- *Inequality* (disruption of human potential through discrimination and marginalisation of people prevented from realising their dreams for an equal chance for safety, security, and self-fulfilment). This needs compassion and empathy from all of us if we are to change things for the better.

- *Digital transformation* (disruption to our way of work and non-work lives, representing both positive and negative outcomes for humans). This requires a dialled-up human response as AI advances, replacing old roles with new ones and demanding a higher order of emotional intelligence from our leaders.

- *Trust* (disruption in the form of the global erosion of trust). This requires a massive, long overdue response from our political leaders and those who lead in the public, private and not-for-profit sectors – trust is at an all-time low and is on life-support: it requires urgent action.

All of these areas require critical leadership skills if we are to stand a chance of changing things for the better.

And across all of these areas, we have seen in *Expert Humans* an approach that is accessible and meaningful to all: *Altruism, Compassion,* and *Empathy*, our ACE attributes:

> *Every man must decide whether he will walk in the light of creative* altruism *or in the darkness of destructive selfishness.*
>
> Martin Luther King

> *A human being is a part of the whole called by us universe, a part limited in time and space. He experiences himself, his thoughts and feeling as something separated from the rest, a kind of optical delusion of his consciousness. This delusion is a kind of prison for us, restricting us to our personal desires and to affection for a few persons nearest to us. Our task must be to free ourselves from this prison by widening our circle of* compassion *to embrace all living creatures and the whole of nature in its beauty.*
>
> Albert Einstein

> *We all have* empathy. *We may not have enough courage to display it.*
> Maya Angelou

Here's wishing you well on your own, personal ACE journey.

Michael Jenkins

Singapore

REFERENCES

Accenture, & Daugherty, P. (2018, October 25). *Missing middle skills for human–AI collaboration*. Accenture. Retrieved from https://www.accenture.com/us-en/insights/future-workforce/missing-middle-skills-human-ai-collaboration

Acciona. (2020). Who are we? I Acciona: Sustainable infrastructure and renewable energy. Retrieved from https://www.acciona.com/about-acciona/about-us/

Anderson, B. (2020). *The most in-demand hard and soft skills of 2020*. LinkedIn. https://business.linkedin.com/talent-solutions/blog/trends-and-research/2020/most-in-demand-hard-and-soft-skills

Bain and Company, & Brahm, C. (2018). *Tackling AI's unintended consequences*. San Francisco, CA: Bain and Company. Retrieved from https://www.bain.com/contentassets/a7ebfd741daf44b6905c597bede52de4/bain_brief_tackling_ais_unintended_consequences.pdf

Becque, E. B. (2015, January 29). *Elon Musk wants to die on Mars*. New York City, NY: Vanity Fair. Retrieved from https://www.vanityfair.com/news/tech/2013/03/elon-musk-die-mars

Böckler, A. (2018, September 10). Distinct mental trainings differentially affect altruistically motivated, norm motivated, and self-reported prosocial behaviour. *Scientific Reports*, 8(1), 13560. Retrieved from https://www.nature.com/articles/s41598-018-31813-8?error=cookies_not_supported&code=c18cd5c3-7ba4-4fe0-8454-036a281b2a91

Böckler, A., Tusche, A., Schmidt, P., & Singer, T. (2018). Distinct mental trainings differentially affect altruistically motivated, norm motivated, and self-reported prosocial behaviour. *Scientific Reports*, 8(1), 1–12. https://doi.org/10.1038/s41598-018-31813-8

Brennan, J. (2020, April 27). Empathy starts with curiosity. *Harvard Business Review*, 77(2), 64–74. Retrieved from https://hbr.org/2020/04/empathy-starts-with-curiosity

Bruneau, E. G., Cikara, M., & Saxe, R. (2015). Minding the gap: Narrative descriptions about mental states attenuate parochial empathy. *PLoS One*, 10(10), e0140838. https://doi.org/10.1371/journal.pone.0140838

Businessolver. (2020). State of workplace empathy 2020 special report: What leaders don't know can hurt them. Retrieved from https://www.businessolver.com/resources/state-of-workplace-empathy

Cameron, K. (2012). *Virtuousness and performance: A productive partnership*. Ann Arbor, MI: Stephen M. Ross School of Business, University of Michigan. Retrieved from https://positiveorgs.bus.umich.edu/wp-content/uploads/Cameron-VirtuosnessAndPerformance.pdf

Canaday, S. (2017, June 18). Cognitive diversity: What's often missing from conversations about diversity and inclusion. *Psychology Today*. Retrieved from https://www.psychologytoday.com/au/blog/you-according-them/201706/cognitive-diversity

Cassell, E. (2009). *Oxford handbook of positive psychology* (2nd ed.). New York, NY: Oxford University Press.

Cassidy, J., Jones, J. D., & Shaver, P. R. (2013). Contributions of attachment theory and research: A framework for future research, translation, and policy. *Development and Psychopathology*, 25(4pt2), 1415–1434. https://doi.org/10.1017/s0954579413000692

Chamorro-Premuzic, T. (2012, November 16). The dark side of charisma. *Harvard Business Review*, 16, 110–123. https://hbr.org/2012/11/the-dark-side-of-charisma

Cheung-Judge, M-Y. (2001). The Self as An Instrument - A Cornerstone for the Future of OD. *OD Practitioner*, 33(3).

Cheung Judge, M. Y. (2018, February 6). What more does OD need to do to become a "must have", "desirable" function for organisations? Retrieved from https://www.linkedin.com/pulse/what-more-does-od-need-do-become-must-have-desirable-cheung-judge/

Chopik, W. J., & Edelstein, R. S. (2019). Retrospective memories of parental care and health from mid- to late life. *Health Psychology*, 38(1), 84–93. https://doi.org/10.1037/hea0000694

CIPD, Houghton, E., & Baczor, L. (2020). *Workplace technology: The employee experience*. London: CIPD. Retrieved from https://www.cipd.co.uk/Images/workplace-technology-1_tcm18-80853.pdf

Davis, J. P., & Eisenhardt, K. M. (2011). Rotating leadership and collaborative innovation. *Administrative Science Quarterly*, 56(2), 159–201. https://doi.org/10.1177/0001839211428131

Domingos, P. (2018). *The master algorithm: How the quest for the ultimate learning machine will remake our world* (Reprint ed.). New York, NY: Basic Books.

Edelman. (2020, January). *Edelman trust barometer 2020*. Chicago, IL: Daniel J. Edelman Holdings, Inc. Retrieved from https://www.edelman.com/trustbarometer

Edmondson, A. C. (2018). *The Fearless Organization: Creating Psychological Safety in the Workplace for Learning, Innovation, and Growth* (1st ed.). New York, NY: Wiley.

Eisai Co. Ltd. (2020). *Eisai's hhc philosophy*. Woodcliff Lake, NJ: Eisai Co., Ltd. Retrieved from https://www.Eisai.Com. https://www.eisai.com/hhc/index.html

Expert Humans, & Jenkins, J. (2020, March 31). *Developing global competencies for 'borderless leaders'*. Expert Humans. Retrieved from https://www.experthumans.org/developing-global-competencies-for-borderless-leaders/

Fine, C. (2010). *Delusions of gender: How our minds, society and neurosexism create difference*. New York, NY: W.W. Norton.

Forbes, & Younger, J. (2020, February). The future of work according to WEF Davos 2020: 5 minute summary. *Forbes*. Retrieved from https://www.forbes.com/sites/jonyounger/2020/02/01/the-future-of-work-according-to-wef-davos-2020-quick-summary/#63f5c97c5b2c

Gilbert, P. (2010). *Compassion focused therapy (CBT distinctive features)* (1st ed.). New York, NY: Routledge.

Glassdoor. (2020). Best places to work. Retrieved from https://www.glassdoor.com/Award/Best-Places-to-Work-LST_KQ0,19.htm

Gratton, L. (2014, June 6). Can altruism be good for business? *The Guardian*. Retrieved from https://www.theguardian.com/sustainable-business/altruism-good-business-community

Habits for Wellbeing. (2020). 20 inspirational quotes on leadership. Retrieved from https://www.habitsforwellbeing.com/20-inspirational-quotes-on-leadership/

Hammond, C. (2019). Does reading fiction make us better people? *BBC Future*. Retrieved from https://www.bbc.com/future/article/20190523-does-reading-fiction-make-us-better-people

Hardman, I. (2018). *Why we get the wrong politicians* (Main ed.). London: Atlantic Books.

Handelsbank. (2020). Sustainability. Retrieved from https://www.handelsbanken.com/en/sustainability

Hincks, J. (2018, April 23). Meet the founder of Impossible Foods, whose meat-free burgers could transform the way we eat. Retrieved from https://time.com/5247858/impossible-foods-meat-plant-based-agriculture/

Honigsbaum, M. (2018, March 22). Barack Obama and the "empathy deficit." *The Guardian*. Retrieved from https://www.theguardian.com/science/2013/jan/04/barack-obama-empathy-deficit

Horii, M. (2020, July 1). *The future of work in Japan: Accelerating automation after COVID-19*. Tokyo: McKinsey & Company. Retrieved from https://www.mckinsey.com/featured-insights/asia-pacific/the-future-of-work-in-japan-accelerating-automation-after-covid-19

Human Systems Dynamics Institute. (2020). Retrieved from https://www.hsdinstitute.org

IBM Watson Talent, Guenole, N., & Feinzig, S. (2018). *The business case for AI in HR with insights and tips on getting started*. New York, NY: IBM Corporation. Retrieved from https://www.ibm.com/downloads/cas/AGKXJX6M

Ikeda, S. (2020, February 17). New study suggests security automation will cause dramatic improvements, but also substantial cybersecurity workforce reductions. *CPO Magazine*. Retrieved from https://www.cpomagazine.com/cyber-security/

new-study-suggests-security-automation-will-cause-dramatic-improvements-but-also-substantial-cybersecurity-workforce-reductions/

IPCC. (2020). Summary for policymakers. Retrieved from https://ar5-syr.ipcc.ch/topic_summary.php

Jamieson Consulting Inc, & Jamieson, D. (2020, May). *Understanding use of self (UoS): To bring your best self in service of others* [Paper]. Annual conference of ISODC (International Society for Organizational Development and Change Management, Virtual Conference).

Johnson, R. C., Danko, G. P., Darvill, T. J., Bochner, S., Bowers, J. K., Huang, Y.-H., ... Pennington, D. (1989). Cross-cultural assessment of altruism and its correlates. *Personality and Individual Differences, 10*(8), 855–868. https://doi.org/10.1016/0191-8869(89)90021-4

Johnston, I. (2016, July 21). Altruism has more of an evolutionary advantage than selfishness, mathematicians say. *The Independent*. Retrieved from https://www.independent.co.uk/news/science/altruism-selfishness-evolution-mathematics-princeton-bath-university-a7148471.html

Kohlrieser, G., Goldsworthy, S., & Coombe, D. (2012). *Care to Dare: Unleashing Astonishing Potential Through Secure Base Leadership* (1st ed.). San Francisco, CA: Jossey-Bass.

Kanov, J. M., Maitlis, S., Worline, M. C., Dutton, J. E., Frost, P. J., & Lilius, J. M. (2004). Compassion in organizational life. *American Behavioral Scientist, 47*(6), 808–827. https://doi.org/10.1177/0002764203260211

Kay, J. (2004, January 17). Obliquity. Retrieved from https://www.johnkay.com/2004/01/17/obliquity/

Konrath, S. (2010). *The end of empathy?* Psychology Today Blog. Retrieved from https://www.psychologytoday.com/us/blog/the-empathy-gap/201006/the-end-empathy

Lanzoni, S. (2018). *Empathy: A history*. London: Yale University Press.

Leslie, I. (2020, July 3). Why your 'weak-tie' friendships may mean more than you think. *BBC Worklife*. https://www.bbc.com/worklife/article/20200701-why-your-weak-tie-friendships-may-mean-more-than-you-think

Lilius, J. M., Worline, M. C., Maitlis, S., Kanov, J., Dutton, J. E., & Frost, P. (2008). The contours and consequences of compassion at work. *Journal of Organizational Behavior, 29*(2), 193–218. https://doi.org/10.1002/job.508

LinkedIn Learning. (2019, January). *The skills companies need most in 2019*. LinkedIn.com. Retrieved from https://learning.linkedin.com/blog/top-skills/the-skills-companies-need-most-in-2019--and-how-to-learn-them

Lucas, M. (2012). Cordelia Fine, delusions of gender: How our minds, society, and neurosexism create difference. *Society, 49*(2), 199–202. https://doi.org/10.1007/s12115-011-9527-3

Ludema, J., & Johnson, A. (2018, September 24). Avoid risk, make innovation possible: Psychological safety as the path to high-performance. *Forbes*. Retrieved from https://www.forbes.com/sites/amberjohnson-jimludema/2018/09/24/ avoid-risk-make-innovation-possible-psychological-safety-as-the-path-to-high-performance/#6e5e5c553223

Marlow, B. (2019, January 22). Brands must put "purpose" over profit, new Unilever boss tells Davos. *The Telegraph*. Retrieved from https://www.telegraph.co.uk/ business/2019/01/22/brands-must-put-purpose-profit-new-unilever-boss-tells-davos/

Mascaro, J. S., Rilling, J. K., Tenzin Negi, L., & Raison, C. L. (2012). Compassion meditation enhances empathic accuracy and related neural activity. *Social Cognitive and Affective Neuroscience, 8*(1), 48–55. https://doi.org/10.1093/scan/nss095

McKinsey Global Institute, Manyika, J., Lund, S., Chui, M., Bughin, J., Woetzel, J., ..., Sanghvi, S. (2017, November). *Jobs lost, jobs gained: What the future of work will mean for jobs, skills, and wages.* New York, NY: McKinsey Global Institute. https://www.mckinsey.com/featured-insights/future-of-work/ jobs-lost-jobs-gained-what-the-future-of-work-will-mean-for-jobs-skills-and-wages#

McGough, G. (2012). Pathological altruism; Barbara Oakley Pathological altruism et al; (Eds) Oxford University. *Nursing Standard, 26*(33), 30. https://doi.org/10.7748/ ns.26.33.30.s38

Mindedge. (2020, February 10). Future of work study: 76% of workers at newly automated companies say technology has made their jobs easier [Press release]. Retrieved from https://www.mindedge.com/news/future-of-work-study-76-of-workers-at-newly-automated-companies-say-technology-has-made-their-jobs-easier/

Monster, & Fellicetti, K. (2020). *These major tech companies are making autism hiring a priority.* Monster Career Advice. Retrieved from https://www.monster.com/ career-advice/article/autism-hiring-initiatives-tech

Moore, C. (2019, November 11). *How to practice self-compassion: 8 techniques and tips.* Positive Psychology. Retrieved from https://positivepsychology.com/ how-to-practice-self-compassion/

NASA. (2020). Climate change evidence: How do we know? Retrieved from https:// climate.nasa.gov/evidence/

National Forum for Health and Wellbeing at Work, & Meechan, F. (2017). *Compassion at work toolkit.* National Forum for Health and Wellbeing at Work. Retrieved from https://www.researchgate.net/publication/322404395_ Compassion_at_Work_Toolkit/link/5af553110f7e9b026bcdc1b1/ download

National Opinion Research Center/University of Chicago, & Smith, T. (2003, July). *Altruism in contemporary America: A report from the national altruism study.* Chicago, IL: National Opinion Research Center/University of Chicago. Retrieved from http://www-news.uchicago.edu/releases/03/altruism.pdf

Neff, K. (2003). Self-compassion: An alternative conceptualization of a healthy attitude toward oneself. *Self and Identity*, 2(2), 85–101. https://doi.org/10.1080/15298860309032

Olson, S. (2020, June 24). E-Forum: Will COVID-19 advance sustainable trade? *ARTNeT. E-Forum*. Retrieved from https://artnet.unescap.org/trade/advocacy/e-forum/will-covid-19-advance-sustainable-trade

Owen, N. J. (n.d.). *Charismatic to the Core: A fresh approach to authentic leadership*. Chicago, IL: Science Research Associates. Retrieved from https://nikkijowen.com/shop/book-charismatic-to-the-core/

Parmar, B. (2010). The most empathetic companies, 2016. *Harvard Business Review*. Retrieved from https://hbr.org/2016/12/the-most-and-least-empathetic-companies-2016

People Matters. (2019, September 5). How a new AI-recruiter is impacting business at DBS. Retrieved from https://www.peoplemattersglobal.com/article/hr-technology/how-a-new-ai-recruiter-is-impacting-business-at-dbs-22984

Philippe Rushton, J., Chrisjohn, R. D., & Cynthia Fekken, G. (1981). The altruistic personality and the self-report altruism scale. *Personality and Individual Differences*, 2(4), 293–302. https://doi.org/10.1016/0191-8869(81)90084-2

Philippe Rushton, J. (1983). The altruistic personality and the self-report altruism scale. *Personality and Individual Differences*, 4(3), 293–302. https://doi.org/10.1016/0191-8869(81)90063-5

Piliavin, J. A., & Charng, H.-W. (1990). Altruism: A review of recent theory and research. *Annual Review of Sociology*, 16(1), 27–65. https://doi.org/10.1146/annurev.so.16.080190.000331

Ponemon Institute. (2020). 2020 Ponemon survey report: Staffing the IT security function in the age of automation. Retrieved from https://www.domaintools.com/resources/survey-reports/2020-ponemon-survey-report-staffing-the-it-security-function

Quigley, J. (2014, December 5). Why every business needs a culture of empathy. Retrieved from https://www.gocanvas.com/content/blog/post/why-business-needs-culture-empathy-success/

Randstad Sourceright. (2020, February). Human resource executive: Upskilling is needed, but employers lag. Retrieved from https://insights.randstadsourceright.com/talent-trends-quarterly/human-resource-executive-upskilling-is-needed-but-employers-lag

Richman, K. (2020, May 29). *Our purpose*. The Forgiveness Project. Retrieved from https://www.theforgivenessproject.com/our-purpose/

Ritchie, H., & Roser, M. (2018, April). *Mental health*. Our World in Data. Retrieved from https://ourworldindata.org/mental-health#anxiety-disorders

Roffey Park Institute, & Poorkavoos, M. (2016). *Compassionate Leadership: What is it and why do organisations need more of it?* Horsham: Roffey Park Institute.

Retrieved from https://www.roffeypark.com/wp-content/uploads2/Compassionate-Leadership-Booklet.pdf

Rollnick, S., Miller, W., & Butler, C. (2008). Motivational interviewing in health care: Helping patients change behavior. *Psycho-Oncology*, *18*(1), 110–111. https://doi.org/10.1002/pon.1416

Schlagenhauf, W. (2018, January). BlackRock CEO to companies: Figure out your social mission if you want funding. Retrieved from https://thehustle.co/blackrock-ceo-social-mission/

Seppälä, E. (2019, June 11). Empathy is on the decline in this country. A new book describes what we can do to bring it back. *Washington Post*. Retrieved from https://www.washingtonpost.com/lifestyle/2019/06/11/empathy-is-decline-this-country-new-book-describes-what-we-can-do-bring-it-back/

Sharma, A. (2020, May 14). Uber-fires-3700-employees-over-a-zoom-call-25669. *People Matters*. https://www.peoplematters.in/news/talent-management/uber-fires-3700-employees-over-a-zoom-call-25669

Shaw Mind. (2020). Mental Health and business: The cost of mental health and ways to reduce the impact on business. Retrieved from https://shawmind.org/team/mental-health-at-work/

Sime, C. (2019, April 17). The cost of ignoring mental health in the workplace. *Forbes*. Retrieved from https://www.forbes.com/sites/carleysime/2019/04/17/the-cost-of-ignoring-mental-health-in-the-workplace/#4d7814e93726

Singapore Airlines. (2020). Sustainability Report FY19/20 Investor-Relations/Annual-Report/sustainabilityreport1920.pdf. Retrieved from https://www.singapore-air.com/saar5/pdf/Investor-Relations/Annual-Report/sustainabilityreport1920.pdf

Sisson, W. (2020, April 25). *Under the microscope: Non-profits and corporations in times of crisis*. Geneva: World Business Council for Sustainable Development (WBCSD). Retrieved from https://www.wbcsd.org/Overview/About-us/Our-offices/North-America/News/Under-the-microscope-nonprofits-and-corporations-in-times-of-crisis

Spacey, J. (2020). *13 examples of altruism*. Simplicable. Retrieved from https://simplicable.com/en/altruism

Strauss, C., Lever Taylor, B., Gu, J., Kuyken, W., Baer, R., Jones, F., & Cavanagh, K. (2016). What is compassion and how can we measure it? A review of definitions and measures. *Clinical Psychology Review*, *47*, 15–27. https://doi.org/10.1016/j.cpr.2016.05.004

Super, A. (2015, November 4). Creating Compassion with Amanda Super. Retrieved from https://www.creatingcompassion.com/

Tett, G. (2019, November 22). Workers can learn to love artificial intelligence. Retrieved from https://www.ft.com/content/db0d9936-0c63-11ea-bb52-34c8d9dc6d84

WBCSD. (2020a). *Circular economy*. Geneva: World Business Council for Sustainable Development (WBCSD). Retrieved from https://www.wbcsd.org/Programs/Circular-Economy

WBCSD. (2020b). *Vision 2050: The new agenda for business*. Geneva: World Business Council for Sustainable Development. Retrieved from https://www.wbcsd.org/Overview/About-us/Vision2050/Resources/Vision-2050-The-new-agenda-for-business

Weng, H. Y., Fox, A. S., Shackman, A. J., Stodola, D. E., Caldwell, J. Z. K., Olson, M. C., …, Davidson, R. J. (2013). Compassion training alters altruism and neural responses to suffering. *Psychological Science*, 24(7), 1171–1180. https://doi.org/10.1177/0956797612469537

Wheatley, M. J. (2002). *Turning to One Another: Simple Conversations to Restore Hope to the Future*. San Francisco, CA: Berrett-Koehler Publishers.

WildHearts Groups. (2020, June 29). Our impact. Retrieved from https://www.wildheartsgroup.com/our-impact/

Workday. (2020). Our story and leadership | Workday. Retrieved from https://www.workday.com/en-us/company/about-workday/our-story-leadership.html

World Economic Forum. (2018, September 17). 5 things to know about the future of jobs. Retrieved from https://www.weforum.org/agenda/2018/09/future-of-jobs-2018-things-to-know/

World Economic Forum. (2020). The future of jobs: Employment, skills and workforce strategy for the fourth industrial revolution. Retrieved from http://reports.weforum.org/future-of-jobs-2016/

World Economic Forum, Getz, I., & Marbacher, L. (2019, October). Altruism can be good for business, as these companies show. Retrieved from https://www.weforum.org/agenda/2019/10/altruism-good-for-business-companies/

World Economic Forum, & Gray, A. (2016, January). The 10 skills you need to thrive in the Fourth Industrial Revolution. Retrieved from https://www.weforum.org/agenda/2016/01/the-10-skills-you-need-to-thrive-in-the-fourth-industrial-revolution/

World Economic Forum, & Nonnecke, B. (2017, September). Artificial intelligence can make our societies more equal. Here's how. Retrieved from https://www.weforum.org/agenda/2017/09/applying-ai-to-enable-an-equitable-digital-economy-and-society/

World Health Organization (WHO) (2019, August 23). Malaria eradication. Retrieved from https://www.who.int/news-room/detail/23-08-2019-malaria-eradication

Zapier. (2020, February). Zapier report uncovers gen Z and millennial perspectives on work/careers; attitudes toward the workplace of the future. Retrieved from https://www.prnewswire.com/news-releases/zapier-report-uncovers-gen-z-and-millennial-perspectives-on-workcareers-attitudes-toward-the-workplace-of-the-future-300997393.html

INDEX

Accepted narrative, 62
Acciona, 160–161
Against Empathy, 127
2030 Agenda for Sustainable
    Development, 23
Agglomeration effect, 160
AIBO dog robot, 12
Algorithms, 4
Altruism, 29, 85–86, 97
    in business, 92–94
    darker side, 88–89
    Eisai, 95–97
    Handelsbanken, 95
    in intercultural contexts, 90–91
    kinds, 87
    what next for, 97–100
    and our world religions, 90
    practical activities to promoting, 148
    self-report altruism scale, 98
    in society at large, 91–92
    threads in philosophy and
        evolutionary biology, 86–87
Altruism, compassion and empathy
    model (ACE model), xv, 9, 13,
    27–28, 54–55, 67
    attributes working in combination,
        81–82
    business benefits arising from ACE
        implementation, 74–81
    business reasons for adopting ACE,
        71–74
    implications of neurodiversity on
        workplace and role expert
        humans, 82–83
    leadership skills, 147–148
    mini-case studies, 150–155
    protecting and preserving purpose as
        core to organisational culture
        and success, 146–148
    'weak tie' networks, 67–71

*Altruism in Contemporary America:
    A Report from the National
    Altruism Study*, 91
*Altruism: A Review of Recent Theory
    and Research*, 92, 99
American workers, 6
Anxiety disorder, 75–76
Appreciative inquiry (AI), 134, 141–146
Artificial intelligence (AI), 3–4, 8, 174
    'AI winter', 11–12
    algorithms, 6
    co-existence of humans with, 46–47
    and technology, 5, 7
ASIMO robot, 11
Associations, 133
Attachment
    theorists, 54
    theory, 55, 59–62
Authenticity, 136–137
    importance of, 134–137
Autism Spectrum Disorder (ASD), 82
Awakening Compassion at Work, 108

Behaviours, 92
Benefits at macro-level, 41–42
Black Lives Matter movement, 37
Black Swan events, 30, 159
BlackRock, 92–94
Brand benefits, 79
*Building Sustainability into the value
    chain*, 21
Business
    benefits arising from ACE
        implementation, 74–81
    of care, 106
    reasons for adopting ACE, 71–74
Business Case for AI in HR, The, 168

C-level executives, 41
Can altruism be good for business?, 93

Caring Charisma, 71–72
'Caring SuperTrio', 73
Center for Compassion and Altruism
     Research and Education
     (CCARE), 108
Center for Compassionate Leadership,
     108
Change, xv, 47–48
     at macro-level, 33–36
     at micro-level, 38–41
*Charismatic to the Core–A Fresh
     Approach to Authentic
     Leadership*, 72
Chatbot, 9–11
Cloud Security, 7
Cognitive Edge, 143
Collective feeling, 113–114
Collective noticing, 113–114
Collective responding, 113–114
Compassion, 53, 101, 111
     circles, 115
     collective feeling, 113–114
     collective noticing, 113–114
     collective responding, 113–114
     compassionate leadership, 105–107
     continuum, 114
     deconstructing, 102–104
     developing, 108–109
     organisational, 111–113
     practical activities for promoting, 149
     pre-requisites for, 101–102
     questions, 116
     in workplace, 104–105
Compassion at Work Toolkit, The, 104
Compassion-Lab, 108
Compassionate leadership, 105–107
Compassionate systems and processes,
     115–116
Confederation of British Industry (CBI),
     79–80
*Contours and Consequences of
     Compassion at Work, The*, 106
Corporate altruism, 29–30, 83, 93, 100
Corporate psychopaths, 61
Corporate purpose, 21
Corporate social responsibility (CSR),
     29–30
COVID-19, 39–40
     pandemic, 34–36, 41, 163
Critical leadership skills for disrupted
     world, 155

*Cross-cultural Assessment of Altruism
     and its correlates*, 90
Cultural synergy, 136
Curiosity, nurturing, 133
Customer
     benefits, 80
     customer-centricity, 27–28

Dark Side of Charisma, The, 71
Darwinian theory, 87
Dehumanisation, 7–11
*Delusions of Gender: How Our Minds,
     Society and Neurosexism Create
     Difference*, 135
Descent of Man, The, 86
Digital disruption, xvi, 3
Digital storytelling, 145–146
Digital transformation, 31, 166–169
     compassion, and empathy, 157–158
'Discover, dream, design, deliver or
     destiny' process (Five–stage
     process), 141–142
Disharmony, 51–55
Disruption, 3, 159
     'AI winter', 11–12
     chatbot, 9–11
     dehumanisation, 7–11
     jobs of future, 12–16
     tyranny of algorithm, 4–7
Distress tolerance, 103, 121
Do Well and Do Good ethos, 44
Dorsomedial prefrontal cortext
     (dmPFC), 128
Drive (Pink), 19

Early childhood psychology, 54
Ebola, 35
Edelman Trust Barometer, 17
Eisai (Japanese healthcare group),
     95–97
Eminent Orphans, 57
Emotional intelligence, 13, 171
Emotional Intelligence Quotient
     (EQ), 12
Empathic bias, 126–127
Empathic distress, 121
Empathy, 119, 156–157
     in companies, 123–126
     dark side, 121–123
     decline, 121–123
     empathy-free zones, 120–121

enhancing capacity for, 149–150
in individuals, 127–134
practical activities to promoting,
        149–150
'Empathy deficit', 37
Employee engagement, 26–27
End of Empathy?, The, 122
Endurance chatbot, 9
Erosion of trust, 158, 171
Ethiopia's Nile River dam, 46
Eudaemonic assumption, 80–81
Europe, compassion in, 109
European Foundation for Management
        Development (EFMD), 61

Fearless Organization, The
        (Edmondson), 61–62
Fiery Chariot, The, 56
Financial benefits, 80
Financial Times, 7
Food security, 22
Forgiveness Project, The, 165–166
Friendliness, 68

Gargantuan task, 38
Gender, 135
Generation Z, 8, 25
Gilbert's model, 103
Glassdoor app, 79
Global Financial Crisis (2007–2008), 17
Global health challenges and pandemics,
        47
Global human health, 162–164
        and compassion, 156
*Global Workplace–A Compassion-free
        Zone?, The*
Goals, 24
GoCanvas, 124–126
'Good Health Can't Wait' idea, 20
'Good hearts', 12
Good work, 60
        instruments, 62–65
Google Meet, 166
Green-washing, 21
Groups, 133

Handelsbanken, 95
Health benefits, 74–77
Heme, 22
Hidden gems, 56–59
Human psychology, 51

attachment theory and ACE, 55
attachment theory and safe spaces,
        59–62
disharmony and unpredictability,
        51–55
hidden gems, 56–59
instruments of good work and safe
        spaces, 62–65
Human Resources (HR), 10
Human skills
        in corporate life, 15
        development, 166
Human System Dynamics Institute
        (HSD), 142
'Humanistic workplace', 28
Humanity, 43–45, 68

Impact, 33
        benefits at macro-level, 41–42
        change at macro-level, 33–36
        change at micro-level, 38–41
        co-existence of humans with AI,
                46–47
        implications for mental health and
                general wellbeing, 45
        leadership for disrupted world,
                43–45
        lenses, 45–47
        organisational cultures and change,
                47–48
        'Our house is on fire', 36–38
        working to raising awareness,
                42–43
Inequality, 156–157, 164–166
Inferior frontal gyrus (IFG), 128
Innovation benefits, 77
INSEAD Tokyo Alumni Forum, 70
Integrity, 27–28
International Classification of Diseases
        (ICD-10), 75
International Society for Organizational
        Development and Change
        Management (ISODC), 65

Job(s)
        churn, 6
        of future, 12–16
        losses, 5
Jobs Intelligence Maestro (JIM), 10
Johari Window, 63
John Lewis Partnership, 93

Kimberly–Clark value chain, 43–44
Kindness, 68
'Known–knowns', 159
KrisLab, 151

Leaders, 133–134
Leadership, 136–137
    development programmes, 63
    for disrupted world, 43–45
    style, 55
*Leading the Social Enterprise–Reinvent
    with a Human Focus*, 45
*Lessons of Experience: how successful
    executives develop on the job,
    The*, 59
Local economies, 36

M3TRIX Academy in Germany, 43
Marks and Spencer (M&S), 79
'Master Algorithm', The (Domingos), 4
Meditation, 128
Mekong in South East Asia, 46
Memory, 58
Menstruation, 44
Mental health
    disorders, 75
    implications for, 45
Microsoft Teams, 166
'Mind's Flight Simulator', 132
MindEdge/Skye Learning, 5–6
Mindfulness, 132
Mission, 24
Mission, Vision, Values (MVV), 25
Motivational interviewing (MI), 134,
    144–145
Munchausen's syndrome by proxy
    (MSP), 89

'Natural climate solutions: the business
    perspective', 42
Nature4Climate coalition, 42
Net promoter scores (NPSs), 80
Next Element, 108
Nike, 25
Non-judgement, 103
Non-office-based workers, 40

Obliquity principle, 94
Obsessive compulsive disorder (OCD), 76
Organisational compassion, 111–113
    strengthening, 114–116

Organisational cultures, 47–48, 111
Organisational development (OD), 62
Organisations, xv
'Our house is on fire', 36–38
Own self, 64

Pandemics, 30
Paris Agreement, 42–43
Paternalism, 89
Paternalistic altruism, 89
Pathological altruism, 88–89
Patient Voices, 146
Peer support groups, 115
Perspective-taking, 135–136
Philanthropy, 29–30
Ponemon Institute, 7
Post-traumatic disorder (PTSD), 76
Power of Vulnerability, *The*, 111
Proof of effect, 73
Psychological safety, 78
    at work, 172
Psychology Today, 83
Purpose, 17
    ACE model, 27–28
    in building sustainable future, 17–18
    leaders and managers using expert
        humans mindset, 29–31
    purpose-and-meaning vacuum, 18–19
    purpose-driven companies, 26
    purpose-driven strategy, 26–27
    thinking about, 19
    in work context, 19–26

*Randstad Talent Trends Report:
    Looking to soft skills*, 6
'Ratner moment', 79
Re-stating or revisiting values, 115
Reading fiction, 132
Reading the Mind in the Eyes Test
    (RMET), 128, 132
Relationships, 53
*Responsible Business: How can HR
    drive the agenda?*, 44
RESTORE programme, 165–166
Return on investment (ROI), 74
Roffey Park Institute, 21
'RULE', 145

Safe spaces, 59–62
    instruments, 62–65
Salesforce. org, 26

SAP, 83
Sarbanes–Oxley Act (2002), 18
Sars, 35
Secure base, 54–55, 59
Self, 65
Self as Instrument–A Cornerstone for the Future of OD, The, 64
Self-compassion, 109–111 (*see also* Compassion)
Sex differences, 92
Shaw Mind Foundation, 77
Singapore Airlines (SIA), 150–151
Singapore-and Australia-based Singtel/Optus, 22
Singtel Group, 23–24
Six 'I's® of Innovation, The, 78
Social media, 79
Social networking, 69
Social skills, 14
Socio-emotional skills, 174–175
Socratic questioning, 143
Soft skills, 13
South East Asia (SEA), 45
Stop–Start–Continue approach, 142
Storytelling, 145–146
'Strength of Weak Ties', The, 68
Sustainability, 22, 43–47, 152
    agenda, 40–41
    of planet, 3, 159–162
    of planet and altruism, 155–156
Sustainable Development Goals (SDGs), 23–24, 159–160
'Sustainable Living' brands, 25
Sympathy, 119

Talent fluidity, 6
Talent Management benefits, 77
Technological disruption, 3
Training for compassion, 114–115
Trust, 78
    in politics, 171–172
    in workplace and businesses, 172–173
Tyco, 18

U-Report, 9
Ubuntu, 53
UK-based Corporate Research Forum, 44
United States, compassion in, 108
'Unknown–unknowns', 159
Unpredictability, 51–55
US-based Center for Creative Leadership, 59
Use of Self (UoS), 62–64

Values, 92
Virtual meetings, 167
Virtuousness training (*see* Through compassion training)
Vision, 24
Volunteering, 133

'Weak tie' networks, 67–71, 85
Wellbeing, 45
West Nile virus, 35
Western mechanistic lens, 53
WildHearts Group, 152
'Work Life Shift' programme, 39
Workday, 154
Workdogs, 154–155
Workers can learn to love Artificial Intelligence (Tett), 7
Working from home (WFH), 40, 68
Workplace, 40
Workplace Empathy: What Leaders Don't Know Can Hurt Them, 123
World Business Council for Sustainable Development (WBCSD), 33–34, 42–43, 161–162
World Economic Forum (WEF), 169–170, 173
WorldCom, 18

Yes, You Can Innovate (Turner), 78

Zoom, 166